Presents

Feng Shui

The Learning Annex
with Meihwa Lin

WILEY

Wiley Publishing, Inc.

For general information on our other products and services or to obtain technical support please contact our Customer Care Department within the U.S. at 800-762-2974, outside the U.S. at 317-572-3993 or fax 317-572-4002.

Wiley also publishes its books in a variety of electronic formats. Some content that appears in print may not be available in electronic books.

ISBN: 0-7645-4144-7

Cataloging-in-Publication Data available from the Library of Congress.

10 9 8 7 6 5 4 3 2 1

PRAISE FOR THE LEARNING ANNEX

"Because I'm so busy I really don't have time to take a full semester course on anything. The Learning Annex gives me the nuts-and-bolts information I need in just one night. It's great!"

— Rick S.

"This was my first Learning Annex class and I plan on taking many, many more. I can't believe how much I learned from one seminar!"

— Wendy R.

"What I really love about The Learning Annex is the easy-to-understand, practical nature of the classes. It's information you can use immediately."

— Susan L.

"It's one thing to listen to a teacher on a certain subject...but it's much better to hear from a practicing expert in the field. That's what makes the Learning Annex so special."

— Dave L.

"The Learning Annex offers classes that you simply can't find anywhere else. The range of subjects they offer is enormous."

— Sandra S.

"There's no end to the Learning Annex subjects that interest me. Every single class I've taken has taught me all sorts of new things."

— George J.

"Being in a class with other people with the same interests makes learning a lot easier and a lot more fun."

— Yolanda F.

"I met my fiancée at a Learning Annex class. I don't remember what I paid, but it was worth it!"

— Kenneth J.

welcome to the Learning Annex

The Learning Annex is North America's largest provider of adult education, dedicated to enhancing the quality of people's lives through informative and inspirational seminars. We offer short, inexpensive courses that provide nuts-and-bolts information on a variety of topics, taught by respected leaders and luminaries in each field. The Learning Annex operates schools in numerous major cities across the United States and Canada, and through its monthly publication, it has emerged as a cultural barometer of what is of interest to the American people.

ABOUT MEIHWA LIN

Meihwa Lin is an accomplished feng shui practitioner, teacher, and mentor. She was a speaker at the 2001 International Feng Shui Conference in Zurich, Switzerland and is a frequent lecturer for the United Nations Staff Recreation Council in New York City.

A member of the International Feng Shui Guild and faculty of many professional feng shui schools, Ms. Lin holds certifications from Feng Shui Research Center, BTB Professional Feng Shui Organization, and The Metropolitan Institute of Interior Design. She trained in the Black Sect tradition under Grandmaster Lin Yun and studied classical compass feng shui with Master Yu.

A native of Taiwan, Ms. Lin integrates her feng shui heritage of traditional schools with Chinese astrology and spiritual teachings and practices of the Black Sect school. She teaches extensively on feng shui and astrology, and she has a successful consulting business in New York. Ms. Lin has been featured on television and radio, as well as in newspapers and magazines, including *Fortune*.

Prior to developing her feng shui practice, Ms. Lin was an executive with *The New York Times*. She is the founder and President of ML & Associates and the designer of The Feng Shui Collection By Meihwa.™

She can be reached by email at MeihwaL@aol.com and by phone at 516-747-4796. You can also visit her web site at www.fengshuicollection.com.

ACKNOWLEDGMENTS

I would like to thank the following people at The Writers' Lifeline, Inc.: Ken Atchity, Andrea McKeown, John Robert Marlow, Jaqueline Radley, Rosemary Serluca, and especially Julie Mooney. Also my thanks go to Roxanne Cerda and Cindy Kitchel of John Wiley & Sons, Tim Ryan of Ryan Publishing Group, and Steven Schragis of The Learning Annex.

I am grateful to Grandmaster Lin Yun for sharing his profound knowledge of BTB Feng Shui, and Master Joseph Yu for his generous and invaluable teachings. I am deeply indebted to Melani Lewandowski for her insights and encouragement, and for writing the Foreword for this book. My thanks also go to Barry Gordon, Steven Post, and Edgar Sung.

I am very grateful to countless helpful people in my life for their love and support. To all my wonderful students and clients, I thank you. You are my inspiration.

table of contents

foreword

The Learning Annex Presents Feng Shui is "the resource" to create a more satisfying life. It is practical, inspiring, and direct.

These are exciting and challenging times. Change is the constant from which great opportunity emerges. In these times, you can test your way of thinking and expand in ways not previously imaginable.

Feng shui is the ancient art of placement. It is a tool that provides for clarity, strength, and flexibility. It supports you in your effort to live to your greatest potential. In the 3,000 years since its conception, feng shui has empowered thousands who have had the good fortune to meet the path of a feng shui master.

Feng shui is a vast subject. It requires years of study, contemplation, and experience to grasp the subtle nuances that give power to the work. And it can be applied very successfully with minor changes under the direction of a skilled teacher.

Meihwa Lin is a feng shui master and brilliant teacher. She lives the balance of insight and action to synthesize the teachings and make them most readily available. She is the work!

I had the opportunity to teach a class at the Metropolitan Institute of Interior Design—Feng Shui Training in the mid-nineties, where Meihwa was my student. She was smart, analytical, and committed to knowing the depth of the teachings from all angles. You might even describe her as relentless in her pursuit to know the core philosophy of the teachings.

As her teacher I was inspired, as I know she will inspire you. Meihwa reinforced for me the importance of continuing to forge forward in my own personal journey of healing, learning, and living the work of consciousness and place in order to make this world a better place for all.

You have the good fortune to find this book as part of your journey—or possibly this book has somehow found you. The Chinese say that luck is a combination of the will of heaven, your personal wishes, and how you bring the two together in life. The words and energies of this book make this wisdom accessible to you right now, so that life will flow most fortunately for you.

I encourage you to use this book as a guide. Know that, page-by-page, it will support you through good times and those of less fortunate circumstance. It will nourish your growth both personally and professionally.

I encourage you to meet Meihwa in person, if at all possible. Feng shui is an oral tradition brought most vividly to life in the presence of the master. You will experience the exuberant joy, wisdom, and depth of this captivating teacher.

The Learning Annex Presents Feng Shui successfully transmits the sacred energies passed down from teacher to student over the thousands of years since its ancient origins. It is as vibrant and fresh today as if it were newly discovered.

Melani Lewandowski, M. S.

Master of Eastern Mysticism, and Feng Shui Master

Philadelphia, Pennsylvania

September 17, 2003

introduction

Welcome to *The Learning Annex Presents Feng Shui*. The purpose of this book is to equip you with the basic principles of feng shui so that you can apply them to your home, your career, and all other aspects of your life.

Feng shui is a vast, ancient, and complex discipline worthy of a lifetime of study, but you need not become a feng shui master to enjoy its benefits. After you've spent a few minutes on each lesson in this book, you'll possess the knowledge you need to make positive changes in your life.

Before we begin, I want to offer you two important thoughts. First, if you're going to get the most out of your experience with feng shui, you'll need to put some of yourself into it. Feng shui will work for you even if you don't believe in it, but it's most effective when you couple feng shui actions with feng shui attitudes. Feng shui is only partially about the way you arrange your furniture. It has far more to do with how you orient yourself. You'll see much better results if you maintain a positive, upbeat, generous frame of mind, define your goals clearly (and realistically) from the outset, and keep them in mind continuously. Feng shui is the study of the interaction between human beings and their environments—don't forget as you're manipulating your environment that you are one half of that equation.

Second, please realize that feng shui is not a magic cure-all. If you'll only be satisfied with immediate, extreme results, you're setting yourself up for disappointment. But if you believe that any positive change is better than none, feng shui is for you.

Feng shui is about small, subtle changes over time—it is not about monumental revolutions. You can't change the orientation of your desk, stick a few plants on it, then expect that tomorrow you'll be promoted to CEO. Feng shui is capable of bringing about profound changes, but for the most part it works subtly and subconsciously over time. Expect small changes, and you'll be delighted when the greater ones come along.

Think of the feng shui you perform on your life as a tiny pebble that you drop into a vast lake. At first the effect will be small, almost imperceptible, but the energies you've set in motion will escalate and reverberate throughout your life. If your intentions are sincere and your efforts consistent, you *will* see profound changes in the quality of your life, but you'll witness them taking effect in small, cumulative ways. Drop the right pebbles into the right portions of your lake—and *keep on dropping them*—and eventually the lake should come alive with the reverberations of your efforts.

That's feng shui.

HOW TO USE THIS BOOK

This book is designed to be a "seminar in print," to allow readers to feel as much as possible as though they're attending one of our evening courses. We've divided the book into topics, titled "Lessons," each of which can be read within 10 to 15 minutes. We have designed this book to be completed in a single sit-down reading. Two types of sidebars will help give you additional, fun, and useful information:

- **A Note from the Instructor:** Insider tips from your instructor, Meihwa Lin.

- **Student Experiences:** Words from seminar students—just like you—who are willing to share their experience with discovering the power of feng shui.

what is feng shui?

Feng Shui Explained • How Feng Shui Works • Varieties of Feng Shui • Feng Shui in This Book

Feng shui is an ancient discipline of Chinese origin that shows us how to develop and shape our living and working spaces to best serve our emotional and spiritual needs. Its theories come from centuries of experimentation and tradition; its philosophies draw from Taoism, Confucianism, Buddhism, and, in modern times, from disciplines as diverse as anthropology, psychology, and geology as the following table shows.

FENG SHUI'S INFLUENCES

INFLUENCE	CONTRIBUTION
From ancient Chinese culture	Symbolism, ritual, mythic animals
From Taoism	Balance of elements/energies
From Confucianism	Human interaction with the universe
From Buddhism	Intuition, meditation
From the New Age movement	Crystals, aromatherapy
From modern psychology	Effect of color on mood, powers of the subconscious
From anthropology	Adapting feng shui to other traditions
From geology	Interaction of environmental features

Feng shui (pronounced fung shway) recognizes that our environment plays a crucial role in our well-being, and it seeks to help us both maximize our environment's benefits and minimize the detriments through the careful selection and arrangement of the elements present in it. The goal of feng shui is to influence the effect our environment has on our attitudes, our moods, our health, and our destiny.

Feng shui recognizes that attitude and intention are more like directions of travel than static states of being. Set off on a positive note in the morning, and you'll find it's easier to maintain that upbeat mood. When your mood is good, you naturally attract good people and things to you, which in turn further elevate your mood.

Let's say you want to improve your financial picture. A traditional feng shui remedy for stagnant finances directs you to place several shiny coins on a red cloth in an area of your home that is naturally conducive to thoughts of money. The abundant pile of bright coins triggers associations with prosperity, and the vibrant red cloth works as an intensifier. Red is a universal color of importance: Its presence tells us "pay attention!" Whether we realize it or not, this display of coins on cloth is sending our brains a message. Consciously or unconsciously, we begin to turn more of our energies toward our finances.

Feng shui is:

A way of understanding the universe: Feng shui draws on a wealth of philosophies and cosmologies to explain the relationship of human beings to their immediate environment, and to the world at large.

A means of transformation: You can use feng shui to help you achieve your goals and improve any aspect of your life.

A way to subtly influence your life for the better: Maintaining good feng shui promotes peace, health, happiness, prosperity, and good relationships.

WHAT FENG SHUI CAN DO

Feng Shui teaches that the primary conduit for good fortune is beneficial *chi* (pronounced "chee"), the life energy that swirls around us and
through us. When we arrange our environments and align our intentions
to draw good chi to us, we naturally accumulate vibrant health, excellent luck, and positive attitudes. You can use Feng Shui to:

- Free up energy you're currently wasting
- Focus more energy on important areas of your life
- Reduce stress
- Restore vigor and optimism
- Improve health (when added to proper diet, exercise, and
  lifestyle)
- Aid in goal attainment
- Enhance relationships
- Promote peace

Feng shui's benefits naturally extend beyond you to influence the
people in your life. As you cultivate your own cheerful, uplifting chi,
you're creating a gift you can give to every person you meet. You can
infuse a room with your chi. Have you ever met someone with an effer-
vescent presence who leaves you feeling energized whenever you've
spent time with that individual? Or do you have a friend whose relaxed,
calming demeanor has a soothing effect on your mood?

Your own presence in the world creates a ripple that reverberates
throughout the universe—that's why it's so important that the energy
you give off is positive.

Likewise, any space you create as a conduit for good chi becomes a
boon to all who pass through it. Your family, friends, and visitors to your
home will benefit from the healthy, peaceful, energizing environment
you've created.

FENG SHUI CAN'T...	FENG SHUI CAN...
Make you win the lottery	Improve your finances
Land the lover of your dreams	Enhance your love life
Get you instantly promoted	Boost your career
Cure a severe illness	Promote better health
Help you harm someone	Help you help others

FENG SHUI: WIND AND WATER

Feng shui comes from the Chinese words for *wind* (the invisible chi carrier—you can't see it, but you can feel its effects) and *water* (the visible chi carrier—you can both see it and feel it). Together, wind and water make up most of the earth's ecosystem; their presence is necessary to circulate chi and sustain life.

Wind and water are the two most dynamic elements; their flowing motion is the same as that of chi. These two elements influence us more than any others—without water and air (wind) we cannot survive. Feng shui maintains that these two elements are the main carriers of chi. A healthy flow of both is necessary to bring life energy to homes, workplaces, and individuals. For example, it's generally considered auspicious to live near moving water, but if your home sits too close to a swiftly rushing river, the chaotic energy from this rapid flow may damage and disrupt the flow of energy in your home. A feng shui expert might advise you to build a wall, or plant a row of greenery, between your home and the river to deflect the potentially negative forces.

Chinese symbols for "wind" and "water."

BOTH A SCIENCE AND AN ART

Feng shui is the science of the interaction between human beings and their surroundings; it's also the art of living harmoniously with the environment.

As with any science, feng shui's principles have been developed through trial and error. Few sciences enjoy the wealth of data that feng shui has collected over the centuries since its inception.

Yet there is also an aesthetic, creative, and intuitive aspect to feng shui. Feng shui seeks to beautify, because beauty is necessary for the proper nurturing of the human spirit. And although it operates by strictly defined principles, there is usually room within those principles for self-expression and creativity. In situations where the rules are ambiguous, or where a number of solutions present themselves, some of the best decisions may be made on intuition alone.

Feng shui is *not* magic: Although it has ties to astrology and ancient mystical traditions, it is not in itself magical or superstitious. Feng shui deals with genuine, observable phenomena, like electromagnetic energy and the connection between mind and body, which modern science and Western culture have seldom explored. It also works on our subconscious minds, helping us condition our intentions.

FENG SHUI BRINGS US BACK TO NATURE

Feng shui recognizes that human beings began our existence in a natural setting. Until modern times, the vast majority of humankind lived outdoors. We were in tune with the natural rhythms of the earth, and we lived in intimate harmony with other living things. Today, we live most of our lives indoors, cut off from the energies and cycles that made us who we are. Although our new indoor existence meets our physical needs, it often neglects our emotional and spiritual ones.

Feng shui seeks to restore our connection to the natural flow of life by bringing into our artificial environments more of the natural energies that fed our outdoor-dwelling ancestors. It recognizes that nature is highly organized and flowing, and seldom uses straight lines. It brings these qualities into our homes in the way it focuses our belongings to buffer harsh lines and angles, and to channel the natural flow of energy.

SCHOOLS OF FENG SHUI

Feng shui is an ancient and complex discipline. Over the centuries it has enjoyed diverse cultural influences and branched into many forms. Modern feng shui in America can trace its origins to three main schools of thought:

Form feng shui: Developed during the Han Dynasty (206 BC–219 BC), this school of feng shui looks for protective influences in the shapes of surrounding landscapes and structures.

Form feng shui recognizes that the land around us is shaped primarily by wind and water, and the quality of the chi they carry. Each landform, whether rolling, green hills or sharp, craggy mountain peaks, gives off its own type of energy. Some arrangements of landforms are beneficial and protective; others produce harmful chi. Form feng shui helps us choose a good location for our homes, and can help us modify undesirable land elements in our present homes. It can also be applied indoors to the way we position our furnishings. Many schools of feng shui incorporate elements of the Form method into their traditions.

Compass-based feng shui: Developed in the Sung Dynasty (960 AD–1279 AD), this method uses an 8-point compass based on a numeric system with magnetic north as zero. Each direction has its own characteristics, energies, colors, shapes, and elements. Applying this compass to a home or office can reveal information about the pattern of energy that flows there. Individuals can then enhance their environments with the proper colors, shapes, and materials for each energy area. Compass forms of feng shui often overwhelm beginners—particularly those uncomfortable with mathematics—and as a result, they have not caught on as readily in the United States. Even in China, people often hire feng shui masters to help them interpret the complex system of numbers that affects their lives.

Black Sect, or "Black Hat" feng shui: This relatively new, Buddhist-inspired school of feng shui, originally from Tibet, uses relative positioning rather than compass directions to determine the specific areas of importance within a home.

Your home's layout is determined from your point of view as you stand at your front door. This method is the most popular in the United States.

FENG SHUI TODAY

Most modern feng shui is an aesthetic blend of many schools of thought, with diverse, multicultural influences. Feng shui has become so wide-spread in the United States within the past two decades that it has found its way into any number of diverse fields, and has had layers of new meanings and associations added to it. While feng shui has proven, by centuries of staying power, that it is flexible enough to merge with a wide variety of thought, it does have its own core system of rules; it's not simply "anything you want it to be." Throughout this book, we'll make references to modern applications of feng shui, but we'll steer you toward the principles that have endured the test of time.

In this book we'll place special emphasis on the Black Sect school, but we'll also mix and match popular forms of feng shui, and bring in the essence of traditions often associated with feng shui. The Black Sect school is currently the most popular form, and is probably the easiest one to put into practical use.

student experience

"When I first became interested in feng shui I tried taking a bit from one magazine article and another bit from a TV show. I was just really scattered, and I didn't get anything out of it. Once I invested my efforts in just one school of feng shui, I realized how much there was to feng shui and am now quite devoted."
—Bob, floral designer

We encourage you to learn about all forms of feng shui, and to practice each to see which will be most helpful for you. But we urge you to experiment with only one form at a time. Although many of their teachings overlap, mixing and matching can cause a certain clashing of symbols, if you'll pardon the pun. Particularly if you try to do compass-based feng shui at the same time as the relative-position feng shui, you may find that your areas of concentration become muddled, and the results will be confused at best and harmful at worst. You'll get the best results if you remain clear in your intentions and focus on one school of thought at a time.

FENG SHUI LESSON-END QUESTIONS

Lesson #1:

1. What attracts you to feng shui? What makes you want to learn more about it?

_____

_____

_____

_____

2. What are your personal goals for your work with feng shui? What do you hope to gain from practicing it?

_____

_____

_____

_____

3. What areas of your life need improvement? What do you believe feng shui can do to help you improve these areas?

_____

_____

_____

_____

Other Thoughts:

_____

_____

_____

_____

principles of
feng shui

Tapping the Power of Chi • Identifying Yin and Yang Chi •
Wood, Fire, Earth, Metal, Water • Heavenly, Earthly,
and Human Luck • The Ba-Gua • Enhancing Your
Home's Compass Directions • Identifying
Your Landform Guardians

In this lesson, we'll cover some of the basic concepts that feng shui draws on. What you'll discover here is just a "thumbnail," of course—any one of these topics could take a lifetime of study. But once you've completed this lesson you'll have a working understanding of the principles behind feng shui. In later chapters of this book, we'll take what you've learned and begin applying it to your environment.

You'll encounter these same principles throughout the book in a variety of contexts: chi, yin and yang, the five elements, the three types of luck, and so forth. If this is your first foray into feng shui, it might take a little time before all these concepts begin to come together. But as you work with them and encounter them in your home and workspaces, you'll develop a sense of the way they affect the quality of your life.

At the heart of feng shui is the idea that we can influence the quality of *chi*, the life energy that flows around us and through us, and in doing so, we can affect the quality of our lives. To accomplish this, we have to learn to recognize the difference between good and bad chi, and cultivate the good while deflecting and diffusing the bad:

Good chi: Healthy, beneficial chi moves in graceful, undulating "dragon lines," in the world around us and through our bodies (chi flows through our bodies along pathways called *meridians*). Natural settings filled with graceful curves, uplifting natural light, and healthy, happy growing things (plants, pets, children) are conducive to beneficial chi.

Bad chi: Wherever chi flows too quickly or chaotically, it can harm us, acting as a piercing arrow, a cutting blade, or a tornado-like force. Straight lines, sharp corners, downhill slopes, busy roads, or swift rivers can generate *sha chi*, or killing chi. Feng shui helps us avoid these hazards wherever we can—and mediate their effect when we can't.

YIN AND YANG

Chi is capable of an infinite number of variations. For example, chi flows through the human body along meridians, which can become blocked and cause serious illness. Acupuncturists practice the art of freeing up blockages in our meridians. Various martial arts teach athletes to focus their chi, thus enabling them to perform astonishing feats of strength.

Every human being gives off a unique blend of chi. Each of the eight compass directions also has its own characteristic chi, as do the five important elements: fire, earth, water, wood, and metal. But all of chi's infinite varieties come down to a combination of yin and yang, the two fundamentally different types of chi.

Taoist yin/yang symbol.

YIN AND YANG CHARACTERISTICS

YANG	YIN
Male	Female
Penetrating	Receptive
Bright	Dark
Active	Quiet
Aggravating	Depressing
Lively	Subdued
Summer	Winter
Growth	Decay
Heavenly	Earthly

You've probably heard the terms *yin* and *yang* before, and have been taught to think of them simply as opposites. While it's true, for example, that yin represents decay and yang represents growth, the two are best thought of as complementary energies. Just as too much decay in a garden leads to a sterile environment, too much growth can lead to an out-of-control wilderness. Thus, yin and yang are most beneficial when they are balancing each other. At any given moment, yin might dominate yang in a particular situation, but such domination is a temporary thing. The two forces are a constant, cyclical balancing act for each other. What's most important is not the way they contrast, but the chi that's born of their interaction.

Yang energy is associated with everything bright, upward, male, and penetrating. It's the energy associated with heaven and with life. Yang colors are dazzling: oranges, yellows, and reds. Yang shapes are straight, pointy, and vertical.

Feng shui teaches us to balance yang by adding yin. Any room that leaves us feeling jangled or overstimulated will benefit from adding soothing yin elements: deep, muted colors (especially blue and black), soft pillows and fabrics, flowing patterns. When you're feeling stressed, perform a little personal feng shui on yourself by playing soft, soothing yin music; breathing slowly and deeply; and meditating.

Yin energy is associated with all things quiet, feminine, still, and receptive: the earth, water, winter, night, and death. In ancient times, an entire branch of feng shui was devoted to yin. Because yin was associated with death, the dangerous yin from graveyards, hospitals, military installations, and similar areas had to be deflected and contained for the safety of those who lived nearby. But yin is also a vital, life-nourishing force: it's the primary energy of mothers and peacemakers.

student experience

"No matter how hard I tried, I never felt comfortable in my living room. I had decorated it specifically to be a haven from the stress in my life, but it wasn't working for me; I actually avoided the room. After beginning to study feng shui, I realized that the room was entirely yin. I incorporated some bright, yang elements and now I love spending time in the living room—it's truly inviting."
—Missy, lawyer

Feng shui shows us how to liven up an overly yin environment with a dash of fiery yang: add candles to brighten up a room or dark corner; decorate with touches of vibrant color and active patterns. If you feel depressed on a gloomy day, mediate that extra yin by turning on more lights, dancing to upbeat music, or doing something fun and silly.

Remember that what's important in feng shui is to *balance* the yin and yang of any given area. Yang without enough yin becomes jarring (picture a living room chock-full of nothing but harsh-angled, modern furniture and shiny, glaring colors); yin without enough yang becomes depressing (imagine a dark, soft, overly yin bedroom—a great place to sleep, maybe, but if the flame has gone out of your sex life, an overdose of yin may be the cause!).

If a room in your home is too yang or too yin for its function, you can adjust the color, light, and décor to bring in more of the missing element and tone down the dominant element. Add soothing yin to a room, for instance, with soft pillows and pastels; bring a touch of active yang by adding brightly colored artwork and accents.

Neither yin nor yang is better than the other; neither is dominant. They can only exist in relationship to each other, and as the classic Taoist symbol represents, even in the heart of yang there's a splash of yin, and vice versa.

YIN AND YANG ROOMS

MOSTLY YANG	MOSTLY YIN
Living rooms	Bedrooms
Recreation rooms	Bathrooms
Kitchens	Reading rooms
Dining rooms	Storage rooms

WHAT MAKES A ROOM MORE YANG OR YIN?

MORE YANG	MORE YIN
Bright, sharp colors	Dark, muted colors
Bright, focused light	Soft, muted light
Stimulating, shiny texture	Soft, smooth textures
Straight lines	Curving lines
Wide open spaces	Small, private niches

WOOD, FIRE, EARTH, METAL, WATER: FIVE VITAL CHI ENERGIES

We've just explored some of the ways that yin and yang, two distinct varieties of chi, can influence a given environment. Yin and yang are mutually reinforcing: We couldn't understand yin without comparing it to, and understanding its effect on, yang—and vice versa. Feng shui sees all the energies of the universe in terms of this fundamental interaction. Every form of feng shui also recognizes the importance of the five elements. Their energies, like yin and yang, complement and affect one another and, in turn, affect the world around them.

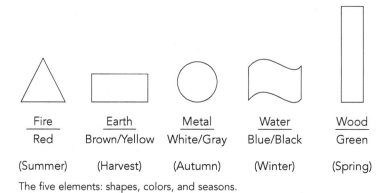

Fire	Earth	Metal	Water	Wood
Red	Brown/Yellow	White/Gray	Blue/Black	Green
(Summer)	(Harvest)	(Autumn)	(Winter)	(Spring)

The five elements: shapes, colors, and seasons.

Every feng shui method teaches that five key elements affect our lives: fire, water, wood, earth, and metal. These five elements can affect us physically (when they're present in our environment) or symbolically (with the presence of objects, images, and colors that suggest them).

In this section, we'll present each of the five elements in a table like the one that follows. Note that the table for each element contains only those entries that are relevant.

Key use	The primary benefit this element offers.
Other uses	Secondary benefits.
Summary	Brief description of the element, its movement, its role in our lives, etc.
Symbolized by	The element's key symbolism: colors, shapes, seasons, etc.
Relationship to other elements	The element it nurtures; the element it controls.
Associated body part	The organ most affected by this element.
Warning	Important things to keep in mind as you work with this element.

FIRE ELEMENT

Key use	Helps you cope with change.
Other uses	Ignites and "turns up the heat" on any area of your life that needs a powerful yang wake-up.

Summary	The most yang of the five elements, fire shoots upward, increasing and intensifying. Fire is synonymous with power, wealth, and recognition.
Symbolized by	Triangles, candles, bright lights, and the color red. Its season is summer, the time of intense heat.
Relationship to other elements	The presence of wood intensifies fire; water symbolism extinguishes it. Fire nourishes earth.
Associated body part	The heart.
Warning	Use fire sparingly, with caution. A little fire goes a long way, and in the wrong combinations and the wrong places, it can be hazardous.

WATER ELEMENT

Key use	Helps you adapt and express your feelings.
Summary	The most yin element, and the most powerful of the five in feng shui terms, water can be a great benefit or a deadly hazard. Where it flows gently and serenely, it can symbolize the flow of wealth, relationships, and opportunity. Water is so vital to chi flow that an entire subdiscipline, Water feng shui, is devoted to it.
Symbolized by	Fishbowls, ponds, and fountains bring the cleansing and accumulative powers of water to areas of your life. Fountains that have water pooling visibly are powerful symbols of accumulating wealth—just be sure that all fountains flow toward the center of your home. Water shapes undulate gently. Water's colors are dark blue and black; its season is winter.
Relationship to other elements	Metal accentuates water symbolism, but earth blocks its flow. Water nourishes wood.
Associated body part	The kidneys.
Warning	Where it stagnates, leaks away, or rushes too quickly, water can be the cause of missed opportunities.

WOOD ELEMENT

Key use	Helps you stick to your principles.
Summary	The preeminent symbol of living, growing energy. Full of vibrant, healthful chi, wood is the only one of the five elements with a life of its own.
Symbolized by	Wood, springtime images, green plants, and blooming flowers are natural enhancers in any area where we wish to experience growth and motivation. Bring wood energy into an area by filling it with healthy plants, the color green, and furnishings made of wood—particularly those with a tall, upright shape.
Relationship to other elements	Water nourishes wood, but metal cuts it. Wood nourishes fire.
Associated body part	The liver.

EARTH ELEMENT

Key use	Keeps you grounded and secure.
Other uses	Restful, peaceful earth energy safeguards our health and fosters good relationships.
Summary	Earth chi is deeply centered. It moves slowly, steadily, and predictably, the way our planet does.
Symbolized by	Yellows and earth tones, and squares and rectangles. To enhance earth chi, place crystals, ceramics, statuary, or pots of stones in your home, particularly at its center.
Relationship to other elements	Fire nourishes earth. Avoid putting wood in earthy locations—burrowing roots can displace it.
Associated body part	The stomach.

METAL ELEMENT

Key use	Hones your focus; aids communication.
Summary	Cold, precise, unyielding metal symbolizes details, plans, and communications.
Symbolized by	The color white, spheres, and domes. Place metal sculptures, furniture, fixtures, and décor in areas where you wish to enhance clarity and boost communication—it's especially good in offices. Autumn is the season associated with metal.

Relationship to other elements	Don't place too much fire symbolism near it; fire can temper metal and make it stronger, but it can also melt it. Earth nourishes metal.
Associated body part	The lungs.

Feng shui teaches us to use these elements to foster the environments we need, as in the following examples:

Fire: If you feel as though life is passing you by, as though you're not receiving the recognition you deserve, you can attract more fame energy by tapping into the power of fire. Light more candles, surround yourself with artwork depicting fire and flames, and decorate with reds and triangular shapes. You can also call the power of fire energy to you with images and symbols of summertime, fire's season. If you suffer poor heart health, you may need to adjust the presence of fire in your environment. Too much or too little can both be hazardous. If your home is full of fiery symbols, your heart ailment may be soothed by removing some of the fire energy, or by countering it with water, fire's "controlling" element.

Water: The element of knowledge, wisdom, and discourse, water can help you clarify your thinking, deepen your understanding, and facilitate your connection to others. It's also naturally associated with good health. Particularly if you have kidney trouble (since water is associated with the kidneys), you'll find that adding real or symbolic flowing water to your environment may improve your health. Too much flowing water, particularly if it's moving fast, can be dangerous, and water that's "leaking" or draining away can take your good chi with it. Keep water under control by adding earth symbolism in areas with an excess of flowing water energy.

Wood: This is a great element to bring into the environment of children, since it complements and enhances their growing spirits. Given that wood symbolizes benevolence, growth, vitality, and adherence to principles, its presence in your home will foster those qualities in your family. Tap into wood energy with live houseplants and green décor. Hang artwork depicting scenes of spring, wood's season.

Earth: Use the power of the earth element to create a more stable, nurturing environment, and to enhance your own ability as a caregiver. Bring an earthy quality to your home with browns and yellows.

Metal: Firm, crisp, and precise, metal possesses all the qualities we want to have when we communicate, plan, and work with details. Bring more metal (and metal symbols—white and metallic colors, circles, spheres, and domes) into your environment, and you'll receive a natural boost to your communication and planning efforts.

How They Interact

These five elements interact with one another in nourishing or controlling ways. When you place these elements—or objects, colors, shapes, or symbols that represent them—near one another, you're either nurturing or disrupting their beneficial qualities.

Some feng shui schools describe the relationship between each of these elements as that of a parent and child, based on which element feeds which: Fire, which needs wood for fuel, is said to be the child of wood; earth is the child of fire (as in volcanoes); metal, mined from the ground, is the child of earth; water is the child of metal (presumably because molten metal can turn to liquid). In practice, this means it's generally a good thing to put fire near earth, because it will enhance, or "feed" the earth, and so forth.

On the other hand, just as each of these elements has a beneficial relationship to one another, each one can control another: metal cuts wood; wood displaces earth, and so forth. If you're trying to cultivate the benefits of one particular element, you'll need to remove excessive amounts of the element that harms it, or the offending element may cancel out the beneficial effects.

CONTROLLING	NOURISHING
Water controls fire	Water nourishes wood
Fire controls metal	Wood nourishes fire
Metal controls wood	Fire nourishes earth
Wood controls earth	Earth nourishes metal
Earth controls water	Metal nourishes water

Elemental Personalities

Even our personalities are associated with particular elements. Chinese astrology recognizes that certain elemental personality types are assigned to us at the moment of our birth, according to the time we were born. Each human being manifests at least some aspect of all five elements, but in each of us, one element is dominant.

Unlike much of the feng shui in this book, the elements that govern our personalities aren't something we can change. They were "stamped" upon our identities at our births. We'll go into this subject in much greater detail in Lesson 11, but for now, here is a brief description of the personality types associated with each element:

Fire people are communicative, passionate, lively, and sensual. They're susceptible to anxiety. Metal makes them feel trapped; wood energizes them. A little water keeps them under control.

Water people are insightful, introspective, restless, independent, and enigmatic. They're slow to anger but can become a tsunami once aroused. Too much earth makes them feel stuck; wood helps them open up.

Wood people are honest, loyal, flexible, optimistic, and ambitious, with a pioneering spirit. They can be impatient and intolerant. Fire environments can upset them; wood and water environments nurture their creativity. A little metal keeps them emotionally balanced.

Earth people are comforting, nurturing, protective, and supremely balanced. Earth people make great peacemakers. They often worry and neglect their own needs. Fire energizes them; water and metal make them tense. A small amount of wood can motivate them.

Metal people are strongly analytical thinkers, harshly independent, and often-obsessive order freaks. They can seem unemotional and selfish, and sometimes lack ambition. Fire rejuvenates them; a small amount of earth stabilizes them.

TIEN, REN, TI: HEAVEN, HUMAN, AND EARTH LUCK

We've explored the way energy flows throughout the universe, and the types of energies that can manifest in our environments. Now let's take a closer look at the way these energies can affect our lives.

Feng shui sees luck in terms of energy: When we have good luck, it's a result of beneficial patterns of chi in our environment. These patterns may be imposed on us by the world at large, but we may also generate them ourselves. Feng shui recognizes three distinct sources for the energy that drives our luck: the chi (the particular combination of yin and yang, and the five elements) that was present in the universe at our births, the chi that finds its way to us through our environment, and the chi we generate ourselves.

As you can see from the previous description, the concept of "luck" as it applies to feng shui is different from the way it's used in Western society. Feng shui luck is not random chance; it has nothing to do with the roll of the dice or happenstance. Instead, it refers to the pattern of events that enfold an individual, the abundance or scarcity of opportunities, and the abundance or scarcity of misfortune. To illustrate the differences in these concepts, let's compare them:

Chance: The way things happen on their own; impersonal, mathematical happenstance. Chance can't be cultivated. Examples of chance include winning the lottery or becoming the victim of an accident.

Luck: Fortune; patterns of events and opportunity. Luck is personal and can be cultivated. Examples of luck include choosing attitudes that attract good relationships and opportunities or letting life pass you by.

Feng shui recognizes three sources of luck: heaven, earth, and human beings themselves. Ancient Chinese cosmology represents this triad in three horizontal lines, one atop the other; the top line represents heaven, the bottom, earth, and the middle (symbolizing our dual nature), humankind.

Tien Chai: Heaven Luck

Ancient Chinese wisdom has it that we're each dealt a particular hand of luck at our births. Tien chai, or heaven luck, is unchangeable—there's nothing we can do to alter the fate heaven deals us. Every era, every year, month, day, and hour has its own chi, according to a complex cycle, and the chi under which we're born leaves an indelible stamp on us. Some of us are born into dire poverty, others into abundance. Some suffer severe genetic defects from birth; others are born with robust health, which they enjoy for a lifetime with little effort. Heaven may be unequal in the quality of gifts it bestows, but it is utterly equal in the manner that it bestows them: Not one of us can change the circumstances of our birth.

We can, however, change our ability to deal with, and take advantage of, the hand we were dealt, by how we develop the other two forms of luck.

Ren Chai: Human Luck

This is the luck we bring to our lives through our own attitude and efforts. It is here that we have the most profound influence, here that the greatest part of our happiness and success is determined.

We've all known people who are somehow able to laugh in the face of adversity, who remain upbeat and hopeful in the direst situations. We've also known people who see doom and gloom no matter where they look. Like attracts like; positive attitudes attract beneficial chi, and negative attitudes accumulate harmful, stagnant chi.

Ren chai is the luck we generate through strong character, right intentions, and hard work. In Western culture it's sometimes called the human spirit. Its potential is enormous; with enough determination it can overcome the gravest handicaps.

Ti Chai: Earth Luck

Ti chai (not to be confused with tai chi) is the luck funneled to us through our surroundings. Our environment can be a conduit or a deflector for opportunity. We can alter our ti chai by altering our homes and workspaces to boost our moods and attract opportunity—this is precisely the goal of feng shui. Remember, though, that our ability to

a note from
the instructor

DEVELOPING INTERNAL CHI

Chinese culture enjoys a rich tradition of internal chi cultivation. Several forms of discipline have evolved to help people enhance their personal chi. Few of these forms of study are well known in the West, but tai chi quan and yoga are now widely practiced in the United States. Yoga students condition their chi through controlled breathing; tai chi quan students practice a slow form of martial arts movement that improves circulation and chi flow within their bodies.

effectively improve our ti chai depends on how well we're handling our ren chai. Feng shui can't overcome a truly negative attitude. But positive intentions and effort, coupled with practicing good feng shui, produces profound results.

The Ba-Gua: How Luck Affects Eight Aspects of Your Life

For centuries, tien, ren, and ti have been represented by three horizontal lines: heaven's line is on the top, earth's is on the bottom, and humankind's, appropriately, is in the middle. In any given situation, each of these three sources may be in a predominantly yin or predominantly yang phase. Yang lines are solid; yin lines are broken in the middle.

Philosophers over the centuries have studied the eight possible combinations of these three lines, called *trigrams*. They found that each trigram possessed certain qualities, elements, orientations, moods, and colors. They named each trigram, and developed a complex system of application for them. The *I Ching*, feng shui's main sourcebook, is a cornucopia of complex meanings based on these trigrams. In the *I Ching* and elsewhere, the eight trigrams are paired, resulting in 64 distinct combinations.

But we don't have to get that complicated. We can apply the eight trigrams to our homes with an octagonal arrangement called the *ba-gua* (or *Pa Kua*). The ba-gua divides our spaces into nine areas of emotional focus, based on the eight trigrams plus a central area.

Close your eyes and picture the layout of your home, as if you were looking at a mechanical drawing. Now imagine you're superimposing an octagonal shape onto your home. Place the bottom line of the octagon at your front door. Sketch this on a piece of paper if it helps.

Now imagine that each eighth of the octagon is divided like a pie slice, its lines extending from the center of the octagon all the way out to the walls of your

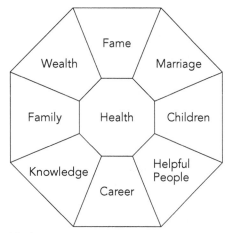

The ba-gua octagon.

home. The area of your home that each eighth of the octagon touches corresponds to a "life area" of the ba-gua.

The ba-gua is oriented according to the front of your home. Your front door may be in the Career, Helpful People, or Knowledge areas of the ba-gua.

Bottom Center: Career

This area is devoted to your life's work, the way in which you serve the world, and typically the way in which you make your living.

Bottom Left: Knowledge

This area symbolizes your ability to gain all types of wisdom and knowledge—including spiritual knowledge. Metal is welcome here, because it supports the flow of ideas and communication. Enhance this area with blue, black, gray, and white. Books are more at home in the Wisdom area than any other.

Center Left: Family

This area symbolizes not only your relationship with your immediate family, but your bond with the larger "family" or clan, community, and humankind. This is a great place for a living room, dining room, or other gathering place. Wood and the color green here represent the living, vibrant nature of a healthy relationship. Avoid fire imagery here; too much of it could lead to arguments.

Top Left: Wealth

This area represents material abundance and financial security. When well arranged, this area enhances our ability to make, keep, and invest money. Green, woody, growing energy naturally belongs here, symbolizing vigorously growing finances. Jade, "money plants," and bamboo work extremely well here. A cheerily flowing fountain is a spectacular idea for your Wealth area, especially if the water collects where you can see it, reminding you of the way your money is accumulating. But make sure this fountain flows toward the center of your house—you don't want your hard-earned dollars draining away!

Top Center: Fame

In this portion of your home, the focus is on your reputation in the world at large, the way others see you. This is a great location for a fireplace. Inflame the Fame area with fiery symbolism to help you bolster your public image. But remember the lesson of ren and ti, and bear in mind that your reputation is what you make it—feng shui can only augment your efforts.

Top Right: Relationships

Here, the focus is on your interaction with the most important people in your life. This is the haven for your marriage, or if you're seeking romance, it's the place to concentrate your efforts on drawing a relationship to you. A home office here is a boon to a business partnership. Decorate with reds and pinks. A little fire symbolism can inflame passion, but don't overdo it or the conflagration could ignite into a quarrel.

Center Right: Children

If you're a family person, this area is devoted to your progeny; whether or not you're a parent, this is the focal point for your creativity. This is where you nurture your ideas—and your offspring. Children's bedrooms are ideal here, as is a home office or studio if you're in a creative field. This is the domain of metal; enhance it with white, gray, and silver.

Bottom Right: Allies, or Helpful People

This area represents the doorway through which your luck arrives, brought to you by the helpful people in your life: friends, mentors, teachers, neighbors, and beneficial business associates.

Center: Health

At the center of your home is the tai chi, the heart of the ba-gua. This is the area that represents the health of all the members of your household. The feng shui of this area is crucial. Earth is the dominant element here. Nourish the center of your home with earthy imagery and colors: yellows, browns, ceramics, and crystals. Don't put too much wood in this area, since wood controls earth.

IDENTIFYING YOUR LANDFORM GUARDIANS

Where the ba-gua is primarily concerned with the inside of your home, Form feng shui examines the patterns of chi flowing through the landscape outside your home. All major schools of feng shui, including the Black Hat Sect, practice Form feng shui to some degree.

In this form we look at the prevalent effect chi has on the landscape around your home. Certain types of chi create specific landforms, which can be advantageous or disastrous, depending on their arrangement.

Ancient feng shui masters linked landforms to four mythical Chinese guardians:

The Black Tortoise: The most important of the four guardians, the black tortoise is usually a soft, curved hill, stone, or mound of trees. A home needs a tortoise behind it to watch its back. Nearly any strong, gentle landform or building behind your home can serve as your tortoise, so long as it's higher than your house and not oppressive. You can plant trees or build structures to serve as your tortoise if you don't have one, but this is the one guardian that no home should be without.

The Green Dragon: To the left of your house as you gaze out your front door, find a gently undulating green hill or line of trees. This is your green dragon, a vital symbol of good fortune and protection in Chinese culture. If you're missing a green dragon, plant a line of fluffy bushes.

The White Tiger: To the right of your home, find an outcropping of white stone or a whitish building. Create a white tiger if you're missing one with a metal sculpture or white stone wall.

The Red Bird: The houses with the best feng shui also have a low hill or low red wall in front, to buffer the impact of the outside world, with a broad expanse opening on its far side—presumably to allow the bird to take flight. The bird is perhaps the least important of the four guardians, but it is also the easiest to install if it's missing. Build a low red wall or redwood fence in front of your home to serve as your red bird, if you can't find a natural one.

Houses with ideal feng shui are said to be resting in an "armchair": They have a high tortoise form at their back, a lower dragon and tiger at the sides as "armrests," and an even lower red bird "footrest" in the front. Best of all is a home that overlooks gently flowing water from its armchair position.

Every method and school of feng shui attempts to maximize each environment's unique potential by modifying or enhancing its chi. Feng shui can be either preventive (in choosing the best sites and arranging them to serve the existing chi) or remedial (by identifying specific problems—like blocked, harmful, or imbalanced chi, or conflicting elements—and performing adjustments). Its ultimate aim is to balance the energies and promote a harmonious flow of healthy chi. Personal feng shui functions in the same way and has the same goals: to cultivate the individual's chi to maximize opportunities for success.

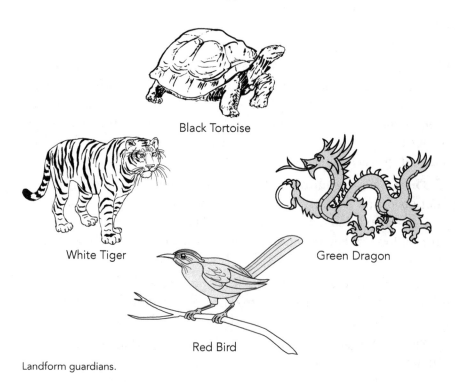

Black Tortoise

White Tiger

Green Dragon

Red Bird

Landform guardians.

FENG SHUI LESSON-END QUESTIONS

Lesson #2:

1. How would you characterize your personal chi?

    ___ primarily yin

    ___ primarily yang

    ___ balanced

2. Which of the five elements in your personal chi do you believe are strongest? Which are weakest?

    _____

    _____

    _____

    _____

    _____

3. Sketch or describe your home here. Identify its eight ba-gua areas.

    _____

    _____

    _____

    _____

    _____

4. Describe landforms or structures around your home that might serve as your four guardians:

    Rear: black tortoise

    _____

    _____

    _____

Left: green dragon

_____

_____

_____

Right: white tiger

_____

_____

_____

Front: red bird

_____

_____

_____

how to use feng shui

The Fundamental Uses for Feng Shui • Feng Shui Cures • Feng Shui Tools

FENG SHUI BY CHOICE

The most powerful way to apply feng shui to your life is by allowing it to guide your choices. It's easier to start off on the right foot than to amend undesirable situations later on. Feng shui can help us select the most beneficial attitudes, associations, life paths, and lifestyles. It can be used to choose a new home or workplace, or to select the best building site and building plan.

To practice feng shui by choice, start by examining your own goals and motivations. What is most important for you to accomplish? You will make much better choices about your external world when you've put some effort into understanding and cultivating your own personal chi. The clearer you can make your own goals, the better informed your choices will be.

Once you've defined your own goals, you can add your specific needs to the general principles of good feng shui. You can choose the people, workplace, and home that have good chi to begin with, and that also suit your individual needs. For example, if you have six kids, you'll need a large home with good chi, plus a good Family area and a flexible Children area. If you're in a creative field, choose a home whose surroundings and overall chi stimulates your creativity, and that has powerful potential in its Children and Fame areas.

In addition to objective, observable criteria, pay attention to your intuitive reactions to people and places: How do they make you feel? Drained or energized? Tense and constricted, or calm and expanding? Black Sect feng shui in particular makes use of our intuitive abilities, stating that if it feels right to you, it probably is.

But proceed with caution: Our impatience and our desires can lead us to override our deeper feelings. Don't ignore that quietly nagging little voice that's trying to tell you something just because you're attracted to a particular choice. A truly right choice brings a sense of peaceful, calm expansion. There's usually a feeling of relief, of things clicking into place. Wait for that sensation, and don't let your impatience choose for you.

But in certain circumstances, choice isn't an issue. We can't always avoid negative chi. We all have to deal with difficult people and contentious situations in both our personal and professional lives. The best thing we can do at these times is to keep our own personal chi healthy and serene so that it's capable of withstanding daily stress. Yoga, tai chi, regular rest and exercise, a high-quality diet, and a positive outlook are your best defenses against stressful situations, because they're the best ways to keep your chi balanced (your chi is balanced when yin and yang are in harmony—see Lesson 9 on feng shui and health for more details). When your body and mind are in balance, your ability to handle difficult people will be improved.

FENG SHUI BY CHANGE

Feng shui can also help you remedy and enhance existing situations and environments. You can make the most of your existing career or home, solve specific problems, deflect negative energies, and boost the power of particular areas of your home and workplace.

This requires a long, realistic assessment of your current attitudes, lifestyle, home, and workplace, with an eye toward changing to harmonize with your goals. On a personal (ren chai) level, this means taking an assessment of your life, identifying weak areas and clarifying your intentions for the future, and then adjusting attitudes and behaviors accordingly. In an environmental (ti chai) sense, this means de-cluttering, cleaning, rearranging, amending, repairing, enhancing, or adjusting the physical spaces in which you work and live. We'll delve more deeply into these issues in Lesson 4.

student experience

Once I clearly identified problem areas in my home, I was able to employ several Feng Shui remedies. They really caused a ripple effect. I felt better in my home, woke up more refreshed and at peace to face the upcoming day, and it even seemed contagious; people around me seemed to be more friendly and energetic."
—Carl, golf pro

FENG SHUI REMEDIES

Feng shui is often used as a remedial measure, applied to specific symptoms or problem areas. For example, if your career and finances are languishing, and you feel that life is passing you by, a feng shui expert would examine your front door: Is it clear, well lit, inviting? How easy is it for people, opportunities, and dynamic chi to find you? If your entryway, the "mouth of chi," is cluttered or in disrepair, the remedy

a note from the instructor

HOW TO CLEANSE AND BLESS YOUR HOME WITH FENG SHUI

1. Clean, repair, and de-clutter the area thoroughly to prepare it for its "new life."
2. Purify it with a cleansing ritual of uplifting music and/or prayer.
3. Invoke the blessing and protection of your Higher Power, based on your religious background.
4. Seal the blessing by placing a focal point in the area: a fountain, altar, statue, or other symbolic figure.

involves cleaning and fixing it. If portions of your home are bombarded by chaotic, fast-moving or negative energy, you can deflect, absorb, or diffuse it with a variety of remedies.

Conflicting symbols in your life areas can cause a variety of problems—for example, if you're struggling to gain recognition, check to see if you've inadvertently placed water (or water symbolism) in your Fame area, which should be dominated by fire imagery.

You can also use feng shui remedies to clear the air of negative chi caused by arguments or harmful people. Some remedies take the form of elaborate rituals; others are as simple as clapping, dancing, playing uplifting music, or filling the affected area with the laughter of happy children.

ELEMENTAL HOME CURES

PROBLEM	SOLUTION
Overheated, tense	Reduce fire symbols; add water
Drafty, unstable	Reduce wood; add earth
Stagnant, dull	Reduce earth; add wood
Damp, cold	Reduce water; add fire
Dry, stuffy	Reduce metal; add water

Feng Shui Tools

As you perform feng shui enhancements and remedies to your environment, you'll find certain objects extremely helpful. These are some of the items that can help you enhance the flow of beneficial energy in your home and office, and will subtly enhance your personal chi:

Plants and flowers: Green, growing plants radiate vibrant, natural energy. Even artificial plants can help. Cut flowers work too—as long as they're fresh—and they can add a lively splash of mood-enhancing color. Plants are a natural remedy for stale, dark areas where chi stagnates, and as buffers for attacking chi.

Mirrors: Mirrors redirect energy and keep it moving; they also magnify the benefit of anything reflected in them—they're great behind plants and candles. Use them to brighten and energize small, dark areas and to deflect attacking chi. If your neighbors neglect their home's appearance, try hanging a small mirror on the side of your house that faces theirs. Feng shui practitioners who have tried this report dramatic improvements in their own moods. You may even find that your neighbors are inspired to clean up their act!

Bells and wind chimes: Their soft ringing diffuses harmful energy and disperses beneficial chi with ripples of cheerful, soothing sound. Brass bells and chimes work best. Position them so that the wind will stir them, where the opening and closing of a door will brush them, or where you can ring them with your fingers as you pass.

Mobiles, windsocks, flags, and pennants: The colorful twirling and flapping from these objects can diffuse harmful chi. Place them between your home and chaotic potential threats like busy roads, railroad tracks, and rushing water.

Crystals: Both natural and human-made crystals reflect and disperse color and light. Hang them above your bed to deflect harmful energies while you sleep, and in stagnant places to enhance positive energies.

Candles: Candles add fiery yang energy, but of a mild, muted kind. Candles ignite passion and, when placed in your Fame area, can help enhance your reputation.

Aromas: The perfume of incense, essential oils, flowers, and dried herbs can greatly enhance mood. Lemon, rosemary, and pine are good for cleansing bad chi. Lavender and violet add a calming yin presence.

Water: A powerful feng shui tool, rich in symbolism, water stimulates chi flow when running, and calms the mind and spirit when still. The best fountains flow toward the center of your home and form a visible pool. Any clean, clear water is good for health, as long as it's not flowing away from your home.

Fish: The presence of fish adds a soothing, living energy. Their constant, undulating motion mimics the flow of good chi.

Music: Almost any kind of music affects an area's chi—and that of the people in it. Choose music that matches the mood you're trying to cultivate. Recorded music works, but live music is the most powerful. Even drumming, clapping, and chanting is extremely effective.

Yourself: You're a powerful source of chi. You can enhance the chi in an area—and influence it in others—by thinking positive thoughts and radiating them into a room.

Feng shui symbolism: Feng shui often makes use of a rich cultural tradition of Chinese symbols to enhance intentions and attract certain types of chi. For example, the image of a dragon clutching a pearl is a powerful wealth attractor, as is a three-legged toad on a mound of coins. Figurines, artwork, and other décor items featuring these symbols can work for you even if you have no background in their meaning, although their power is enhanced to the degree that you're familiar with what they stand for.

 a note from
the instructor

TRADITIONAL CHINESE SYMBOLISM

Many feng shui books recommend that you place a figurine of a three-legged toad clutching a coin in its mouth in areas of your home devoted to wealth and finances. The symbolism behind this object requires a little explanation: Centuries ago, Liu-hai the Immortal (a figure from Chinese folklore) discovered a toad trapped in a village well. The toad could not hop out of the well because it was missing a hind leg. The philosopher rescued the toad from the well. In gratitude, the toad brought the philosopher a single coin in its mouth, from a hidden stash of treasure, each day for the rest of its life, until Liu-hai became wealthy. The three-legged toad figurine honors this story and represents a steady stream of wealth on its way to you.

Three-legged toad figurine.

But you don't have to stick to Chinese symbols. You can use traditional American symbols, or borrow from any cultural tradition you like—or perhaps best of all, create your own symbols.

FENG SHUI LESSON-END QUESTIONS

Lesson #3:

1. List, as specifically as possible, your five most important goals for the future:

_____

_____

_____

_____

_____

2. If you could change any five things about your life, what would you change?

_____

_____

_____

_____

_____

Other Thoughts:

_____

_____

_____

_____

_____

applying feng shui to your home

Boosting Your Health and Attitude by Improving Your Home's Chi • Choosing and Enhancing Your Home's Design and Décor • Targeting and Adjusting Your Home's Trouble Spots

Feng shui teaches that your home symbolizes your body. Its walls are your skin; its plumbing, your digestive system; its bedroom, your relationships. Your house's condition and the quality of its chi are synonymous with your own.

Similarly, your home symbolizes your goals, dreams, and needs. A home with good feng shui fosters our deepest needs, such as our need to feel that we're in a safe, well-delineated space that is uniquely our own, our need for centeredness, and our need for gathering spaces.

We're conditioned to think about what our home says to others about us, but feng shui is much more concerned with what our home says to *ourselves* because frequently repeated thoughts become habits. Feng shui teaches us to shape our homes to reinforce the messages we need to hear. We'll spend the next two lessons on this subject. In Lesson 5, we go through your home room by room, addressing issues specific to each area. But in this lesson we focus on your home as a whole, discussing its shape, building materials, and its overall effect on your health, mood, and luck.

FIRST STEPS

Houses with good feng shui have a calm, balanced, uplifting chi, which both soothes and energizes. Chi circulates freely and serenely throughout the house. Good chi flow promotes vibrant health and a positive mental attitude, and invites opportunity and good fortune. As you begin to perform feng shui on your home, work on one room at a time. Take note of its prevailing energy patterns. How does the room make you feel? Is it inviting, calming, and invigorating, or jarring, stagnant, or unsettling?

Strive for a balance of energies in each room. Make its purpose clear. Don't follow fads and fashions; doing so creates stress and tension, and has you decorating your home for the wrong reasons. Instead, decorate to allow for creative expression: yours, and that of all members of your household. This is what truly makes a house into a home.

Give yourself time to think about each room and the potential remedies for it. Give your ideas time to "ripen," because even though there's an intuitive side to feng shui, it isn't productive to act impulsively on something that can have such a profound effect on your future.

Before you begin to rearrange furniture, knock down walls, or redecorate, do the following in each area of your home, as needed:

- **Clean:** Dust and grime is depressing to the spirit and causes chi to stagnate. It's also difficult to form any realistic impression of the state of your home when it's dirty. A vigorous cleaning is often more effective than any feng shui remedy. It's a necessary first step if your feng shui efforts are going to be successful.

- **De-clutter:** In order to clear the way for new energies and opportunities, you need to get rid of clutter. Lao Tsu said, in so many words, that everything you own should serve you; otherwise, you're serving *it*. The state of your surroundings represents the state of your body, heart, and mind. Make your outside world look the way your inner world should—and start by eliminating the dead weight.

■ **Repair:** It's imperative that your environment be in good working order. Next to dirt and clutter, disrepair is one of the worst "downers," emotionally and spiritually. Feng shui urges us to fix clogged and leaky drains lest they interfere with the flow of chi, repair stuck or creaking doors so that good chi can enter and bad chi can be thwarted, replace broken light fixtures, and repair any visible signs of malfunction throughout our homes.

THE FENG SHUI HOME

There's no such thing as a house with perfect feng shui, but certain shapes, construction materials, lighting arrangements, and décor styles are more conducive to good chi than others. If you're in the market for a new home, or looking for ways to improve the one you currently own, the information in the following sections will help you.

student experience

" When shopping for a house, my husband and I just couldn't decide between two homes. We visited each of them several times. We really liked both of them, but something kept drawing us back to one—it just felt better. Now that I've started to study Feng Shui I realize that the home we chose by far had the better Feng Shui."

—Joan, executive assistant

House Shape

The houses with the best feng shui are solid, balanced, and symmetrical. Look for a simple, rectangular-shaped house, with no protruding wings or odd angles. A simple, symmetrical shape means that each area of your ba-gua octagon receives an almost equal share of space. Of course, to be absolutely true to the ba-gua, you'd have to live in a round or octagonal house, but such a house isn't practical.

Avoid homes with asymmetrical or unbalanced architecture. Some experimental, super-modern building styles make the second story appear larger than the first, build on an uneven trapezoid-shaped layout instead of a rectangle or square, or create the effect of several small segments joined together. Homes like these invite negative chi for a variety of reasons. Instead, choose a home that radiates stability, unity, and balance.

What if you're currently living in an asymmetrical house and you're not in a position to relocate? You may be able to lessen the house's harmful effects by planting greenery to blunt harsh angles and by installing outdoor lights to fill in hollows and concave corners. Balance asymmetry with shutters, lattices, or other additions.

Building Materials

Natural materials work best: wood (very yin), stone (very yang), adobe, and brick. Avoid shiny, reflective surfaces (like the glass on some high-rises) or jagged, protruding building materials. Balanced, solid, smooth construction attracts the best chi.

Floors

Solid, natural materials are best for flooring as well. Choose wood for more yin; stone or tile for more yang. The harder and shinier the floor, the faster the flow of chi. Choose a shinier texture in areas of your home that could benefit from an energy boost, but consider a more muted texture in busy areas. Avoid harsh patterns and textures. Most carpets are too full of jarring synthetic fibers to promote good chi flow, but rugs are generally beneficial. The best rugs are those made of natural fibers. Choose muted single-color rugs, or rugs with subtle, wavy patterns for rooms that need a more relaxed, yin environment; pick bright, rich colors and energetic patterns for rooms that require more yang.

Ceilings

A flat or domed ceiling is ideal. Avoid slanted ceilings—they trap the chi. Cover exposed beams, or adjust them by shining lights on them or hanging special feng shui flutes on them.

Walls

Walls should be smooth but not shiny (avoid high-gloss finishes). Avoid walls with protruding corners (as you'd have in an L-shaped room). In terms of colors, soft, muted, yin colors work best for most walls; reserve vibrant yang colors for accents. Solid, mottled, wavy, and floral-patterned walls invite yin energy; stripes, prints, and regimented patterns enhance yang chi.

Doors

All doors should be in good repair, and should open, swing, and latch properly. Two doors should not clash together; this invites arguments. The front door is the most important door in the house, and the ideal front door has no windows, and is red, green, or black. Don't have a mirror facing the door.

Windows

Windows should not be too large or too small: If they're too large, they'll let in too much rushing chi; if they're too small, they won't permit enough chi or natural light to enter the home. Windows should be at least as tall as the tallest family member, but not so large that they dominate an entire wall.

Fireplaces

Fireplaces should not dwarf a room. Avoid fireplaces in the bedroom— their energy is too strong. They can be beneficial in areas devoted to fame.

Lighting

In general, the more light in a given area, the better. Natural light is best, but as mentioned earlier, avoid oversized windows. Windows that are the right size for a given room will let in a healthy amount of natural light, as long as they're clean and well maintained. Avoid fluorescent lights—their cold, harsh glare makes people look sick. Use full-spectrum lighting wherever possible. Alternate direct and indirect lighting; for instance, floor or table lamps combined with wall sconces.

APPLYING THE BA-GUA OCTAGON TO YOUR HOME'S LAYOUT

In Lesson 2 we introduced you to the ba-gua octagon, with its eight vital aspects of your life (among them, Family, Wealth, and Career). In the graphic on the next page, you can see how the ba-gua looks when it's superimposed on a home's layout.

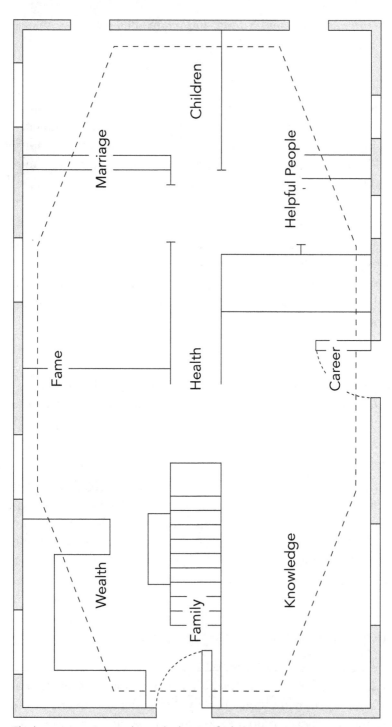

The ba-gua superimposed over the layout of a house.

To correctly orient the ba-gua to your own home, imagine that you're standing at your front door looking in (remember that in Black Hat Sect feng shui, the ba-gua's positioning is relative, not oriented to compass directions as in other schools). The Career section at the bottom center of the ba-gua should correspond with the center of the front of your home. If your front door is in the center of the front of your home, you'll be entering your home through the Career area. If it's to the left, you'll enter through the Knowledge area, and if it's to the right, you'll enter through Helpful People.

Some rooms are better suited to certain ba-gua areas than others.

Here is a list of ba-gua areas and the rooms that are best suited to them:

AREA	IDEAL FOR...
Career	Entry, living room, office
Wisdom	Office, library
Family	Living room, dining room, recreation room
Wealth	Bedroom
Fame	Living room, dining room, bedroom
Marriage	Master bedroom, kitchen
Children	Office, kids' rooms
Helpful People	Living room, dining room, office
Health (Tai Chi)	Dining room, living room

CHOOSING AND ENHANCING YOUR HOME'S FURNITURE AND DÉCOR

Choose furniture that suits the energy you're trying to cultivate: modern, tall, hard furniture is more yang; soft, overstuffed, cushiony furniture is more yin. The beds with the best feng shui have wooden frames and no springs. Metal in beds may cause insomnia. Avoid electric blankets and waterbeds. The best dining tables are round or oval, and made of natural materials.

Decorate with natural materials. Avoid vertical blinds—they cut the room like knives. Steer clear of rough, jagged textures. In general, strive to balance yin and yang.

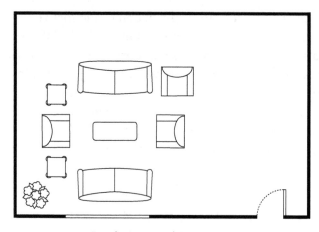

Poorly Arranged Furniture

- Seats in confrontational positions
- Harsh angles aimed at seating positions
- Shape of seating arrangement discourages beneficial chi flow
- Most seats have no tortoise, dragon, or tiger guardians

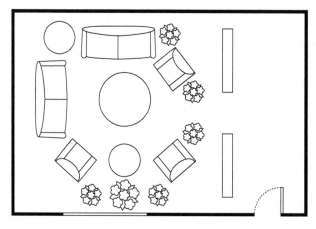

Well-Arranged Furniture

- Seating imitates the ba-gua
- No harsh angles
- Plants deflect harmful chi flowing through window
- Most seats have a tortoise, dragon, or tiger guardian

Poorly arranged and well-arranged furniture.

Arrange your furniture with the four landform guardians in mind: a tortoise at the back, a red bird at the front, a green dragon to the left, and a white tiger to the right. Seating should back up against a strong "tortoise": a wall, freestanding bookcase, or at least a screen. They should have a free bird area in front, and a low table, plant, or other piece of furniture to each side to serve as tiger and dragon.

Chairs themselves can contain all four guardians. Chairs with low ottomans have the ideal bird. High-backed chairs offer the secure feel of a guarding tortoise at the back. Solid armrests form the dragon and tiger.

Tables can be hazardous to flowing chi, unless they're round or oval. Sharp corners can create killing chi. Tables are said to symbolize earth because they passively receive what's placed upon them. Like earth, they should exude stability.

In general, arrange furniture to mimic the ba-gua octagon: Where you can, position chairs and couches to create a symmetrical octagonal or round shape.

USING COLOR TO CULTIVATE CHI

As you're choosing décor and color schemes, you can use color to foster the moods and attitudes you want in each room. You can incorporate colors into a room by painting the walls or adding décor touches such as draperies, rugs, wall hangings, pottery, and other objects. You don't have to go overboard: If a room needs just a slight boost of yang energy, try adding some red or orange candles. If a room is predominantly red, you might choose to add a single blue accent piece (a rug or wall hanging) for balance.

Colors can affect our moods in the following ways:

- **Red:** Attracts, inflames, energizes
- **Green:** Stimulates growth and creativity, invigorates, promotes healing
- **Yellow:** Cleanses, clarifies, resolves, brings moods and goals to full fruition, stimulates health
- **Purple:** Creates an exotic, sensuous ambience; inspires adventure

- **Blue:** Inspires, invites introspection, encourages wisdom
- **Black:** Creates mystery, intrigue; inspires creativity and mobility
- **White:** Invites clarity, precision, perfection
- **Gray:** Fosters secrets, elicits helpfulness

Color is also symbolic; Chinese culture is replete with color symbolism. Apply these colors in the appropriate areas of your home to augment your personal efforts:

- **Red:** Change, power
- **Green:** Growth, hope, rejuvenation, health
- **Yellow:** Stability
- **Purple:** Wealth, royalty
- **Blue:** Knowledge, nobility
- **Pink:** Marriage, motherhood, love
- **Black:** Wisdom, authority, networking
- **White:** Purity, authority
- **Gray:** Allies, secrets

TARGETING AND ADJUSTING YOUR HOME'S TROUBLE SPOTS

If the occupants of a house suffer from chronic ill health, depression, anxiety, negative emotions, poor finances, or unfulfilling relationships, unhealthy chi may be to blame. Changes to the home's layout and décor may improve the quality and flow of chi, unblocking "clogged" areas and restoring proper flow and balance.

Let's look at some common problem areas and their cures:

Missing areas of a room or house: An L-shaped room or house has a piece of a life area, or a compass direction, "missing." You can compensate for these missing areas by lighting the outside space or delineating it with flags; inside you can add mirrors to the affected walls and blunt sharp corners with plants, wind chimes, or draped fabric.

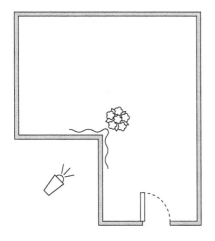

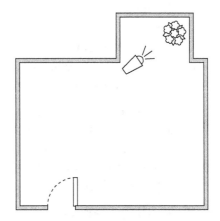

Missing Area/ Protruding Corner:

Cover with drapery or other soft material; place plant or hang crystal ball at corner. Outside: Light "missing" corner

Dead Space:

Aim lights, hang crystal ball, place plant

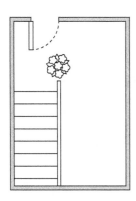

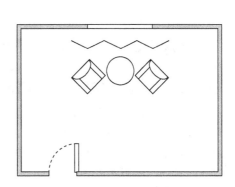

Attacking Stairs:

Place a plant between door and stairs

Remedies for problem areas.

Attacking Chi from Window:

Place plants or screen between window and seats

Odd-shaped rooms: Your home may contain a few rooms with an asymmetrical layout: an L shape or trapezoid shape. Some upstairs rooms in older houses have sloped ceilings. If possible, use these rooms for secondary functions (recreation or storage). Above all, avoid using them as bedrooms.

Concave corners, dead spaces: A small, dark alcove or a corner that is tucked away from the rest of the room can trap chi, disrupting its flow and causing it to stagnate. Get the chi moving again by adding more light to these areas, hanging crystals, or enlivening them with plants.

Protruding corners and "attacking" stairs: A corner that sticks out, as in a protruding closet, an L-shaped room, or a protrusion that hides pipes or ductwork can create a sharp angle that causes chi to flow unevenly. Soften protrusions with plants, fabrics, and wind chimes. The chi flowing down a stairway can accelerate to dangerous speeds. If a doorway lies at the bottom of a staircase, the rushing chi "attacks" anyone who comes through the door. Place a plant between the stairs and the door to absorb the attacking energy.

THE FIVE ELEMENTS: APPLYING THEM TO YOUR DÉCOR AND AVOIDING HARMFUL COMBINATIONS

In Lesson 2 we introduced you to the richly symbolic feng shui five elements: fire, earth, metal, water, and wood. Just as you've been using yin and yang textures and colors to change the chi in various parts of your home, you can use the colors, shapes, and symbols associated with each of the five elements to bring their energy to your living spaces. Here you'll find for each element the energies and attitudes it fosters; the bagua areas in which it's particularly helpful; and the colors, shapes, and symbols that nurture its chi:

Fire literally "turns up the heat" wherever it's applied. It's associated with passion and emotional expression. In small quantities, it can energize a lackluster area, but too much fire can become "inflammatory," leading to hot tempers, arguments, and other excesses. Fire is particularly helpful in the Fame area. A small amount in the Marriage area can add a spark to your sex life. Add fire to your décor with red accents and furnishings, with triangular shapes, and with images of flames and summertime.

Earth is the element of health and nurturing. Earth energy has a soothing effect. Its presence creates a sense of well-being and stability. Earth symbols are extremely helpful in the Health area (at the center of your home). Introduce earth energy to your home with earth tones; with pottery and stone; with low, rectangular shapes; and with images of mountains.

Metal is associated with creativity, communication, and children. It can promote creativity and planning, and help you communicate more clearly. It's particularly beneficial in the Children area of your ba-gua. Boost the metal in a given area by decorating with metal objects, whites, spheres, and domes.

Water is closely associated with intuition, communication, networking, and wealth. Still, deep water represents the accumulation of wisdom; flowing water suggests socializing, communication, transportation, and commerce. Water collecting in a pool symbolizes the accumulation of wealth. Clear, flowing water is an important component of health. But too much water can be hazardous; it can literally wash away good chi, and when water is draining away, it can symbolize luck and opportunities going down the drain.

Use water images in your Knowledge area to help you increase your wisdom. Introduce the energies of water with the colors black and blue, with wavy lines and flowing patterns.

Wood is the element of vibrant life and growth. Its presence is beneficial in numerous areas, especially Health. Bring wood energy to an area with rich greens, tall shapes, and images of springtime and youth. The best way to introduce wood to an area is by decorating with genuine wood: wooden furniture, sculpture, and other décor items, and potted plants.

As we discussed in Lesson 2, each of the five elements interacts with the others in specific ways. Each element nurtures another element (wood nurtures fire, fire nurtures earth, earth nurtures metal, metal nurtures water, water nurtures wood); similarly, each element controls another element (wood controls earth, earth controls water, water controls fire, fire controls metal, and metal controls wood). You can use the relationships among the elements to enhance the energies you're fostering in each area of your home. For instance, if you're cultivating fire energy in your Fame area, you may choose to add some wood to "feed" the flames. But if the fire in a given area threatens to get out of control, you can bring in some water symbolism to keep it in check.

The most important thing is to become conscious of the elements that are present in your environment and be aware of the ways they are interacting. Some combinations can be hazardous (for instance, when you combine equal amounts of fire and water, you get potentially volatile steam). Here we've listed each element with its "control" element, and the steps you can take to alleviate potential conflicts between them:

Wood controls earth: Avoid too much wood in "earth" areas associated with your health (the center of your home).

Earth controls water: Avoid too much earth in water areas devoted to career (the front) and finances (the upper-left corner).

Water controls fire: Avoid too much fire in the area devoted to reputation (in the back), which is fire's domain.

Fire controls metal: Remove excess fire from "metal" areas of communication, helpful friends, and children (on the right-hand side of your home).

Metal controls wood: Minimize metal's appearance in areas devoted to family life (in the center left of your home), health, and wealth.

FENG SHUI LESSON-END QUESTIONS

Lesson #4:

1. List below all the rooms in your home. Describe the chi of each room. Is it predominately yin, yang, or balanced? Are all five elements represented, or is the chi of one or more elements weak or dominant?

_____

_____

_____

_____

_____

2. Describe here any ideas you have for feng shui adjustments you could make to each room. Set this entry aside for at least a week, then re-read what you've written here. Do your ideas still make sense? Develop further the ideas that have "staying power."

_____

_____

_____

_____

_____

_____

Other Thoughts:

_____

_____

_____

_____

_____

_____

feng shui room by room

The Entranceway to Your Home • Feng Shui Advice for Your Living Room, Kitchen, Bedrooms, Kids' Bedrooms, Bathrooms, and Other Areas

Now that we've explored some of the basic principles of feng shui, and we've discussed various ways to apply them to your home, we're now going to take a "feng shui tour" of your house. As we work our way from room to room, we'll explore the specific issues that arise in each living area.

YOUR FRONT DOOR AND ENTRYWAY

Your front door is one of the most important aspects of your home. Your front door is the "mouth of chi," where the house inhales chi from its surroundings. Your front entry should be clear and well maintained so that your home can breathe easily. A good front entry is large, but not so big that it dominates the architecture. Your front door should be easy to approach; guide visitors to your door via a wide, smooth, slightly curved, well-lit path.

You can enhance your front entry's feng shui, attracting more opportunities and deflecting negative luck, by performing the following measures:

- Choose a solid door without windows.
- Paint your door red, green, or black.
- Keep the front of your home well lit and well maintained.
- Lay a wide, gently curving path leading up to your front door.

Maintain an open, welcoming space in the area directly inside your front door. This is your "bright hall," where beneficial chi collects as it enters your home. The interior entry, the first place the incoming breath of chi passes, should be bright and welcoming, and should encourage entering chi to flow deeper into the house.

The first view upon entering a home is extremely important. It's beneficial to see beauty and harmony; it's harmful to see clutter. Make sure no bed, stove, fireplace, or toilet is visible from the front entry—these items are too vital to expose to entering chi. The front entry area should be well lit, particularly with natural light. Bright, welcoming colors such as light pastels will enhance your foyer. Avoid dark colors unless the area is large enough to accommodate them—and even then use them sparingly, as accents.

YOUR LIVING ROOM

Your living room is literally and figuratively the hub of family life and a microcosm of the entire household. The way you orient, arrange, and decorate this room can have a profound influence on your success, finances, friendships, and especially your family life. An inviting living room can enhance goodwill; a poorly arranged one can engender strife.

Because of its significance as a gathering place for the family, the living room is one of the most important places for symbols of good family fortune. But your feng shui efforts here should be subtle; if family members and guests sense that you're trying too hard to cultivate a given atmosphere, your intentions could backfire.

Arrange your living room seating to mimic the flow of chi: place sofas and chairs in an octagonal or horseshoe pattern. Avoid dead ends and corners, where chi may stagnate. Try to provide each seat with its proper guardians: a tortoise at the back (a wall or tall piece of freestanding furniture) a tiger and dragon to each side (other seats, end tables, or plants), and a bird at the front (a coffee table and an open space). Avoid seating people directly across from one another—this may encourage confrontations. Put the largest sofa against the sturdiest wall.

Seat as many of your guests as possible with a view to the door, and offer them the "command position," the chair that gives them a clear view of the door (without putting them directly in line with it) and a full view of everyone in the room, while giving them a solid "tortoise" at their back.

Because living rooms should be predominantly yang, make sure there's adequate, cheery lighting and stimulating décor. Create a focal point for this room: a piece of artwork or other display, either on a table or wall, that draws the eye when a person enters the room. Choose as this focal point something that will serve the symbolic spirit of the room; for instance, in a living room you might choose to display a large, handsomely framed portrait of the family, or a sculpture of a mother and child. One of the best possible items you can place in the living room is a large family portrait in which everyone is smiling confidently. This states symbolically the importance of the family's relationship to the outside world, and emphasizes that the family relates to others as a unit.

Avoid images of aggression in this room. Don't display swords, firearms, military scenes, or fierce animals. A small amount of fire in this room (a few candles, for instance) can be stimulating, but avoid too much fiery symbolism, as it could ignite conflict.

Cure potential strife in your living room by blunting sharp corners, like the ones you might find on certain coffee tables, bookcases, and other pieces of furniture. A carpenter may be able to do this for you if you're not comfortable doing it yourself. Or you might decide to get rid of your sharp-cornered furniture and redecorate with round-edged pieces. If you can't blunt the edges or replace the items, try repositioning the furniture so that the piercing chi from its edges will not affect anyone seated in the room. Drape soft fabric and place plants in front of any corners that can't be removed or repositioned.

YOUR KITCHEN

In ancient times, the family hearth was considered a sacred place. This is where our ancestors harnessed the powerful element of fire to cook the food that nourished the household. Great ritual and ceremony once attended the act of cooking. And even though today your "hearth" may be a high-tech electric range, you're still performing this essential, centuries-old ritual.

The kitchen is the symbolic "stomach" of your home. Because of its intimate connection with nourishment and sustenance, the kitchen area is synonymous with health and wealth. Even from a pragmatic perspective, this is true: The quality of your food affects the quality of your ability to work and gain wealth.

In the feng shui of kitchens, the stove is the main event. The stovetop is the most important aspect of the stove: The exposed heating elements where you place pots and pans symbolizes the fire our ancestors once used for cooking. If your stovetop is separate from the oven, the stovetop, not the oven, is the focal point. Everything else in the kitchen is secondary to this central feature.

Good kitchen feng shui places the stove against a solid "tortoise" wall, which means you're standing in the stove's red bird aspect when you cook. Your stove should not face, or be visible from, the front door. A mirror on the wall behind the stove will reflect—and thereby augment—the bounty of the meals that you cook on it. Respect your stove's vital role in your family's health and wealth by keeping it clean and in good working order at all times.

Your kitchen's layout should reflect the centrality of the stove. Your stove should have the command position in the room (it should be able to "see" the door but not be in a direct line with it, and it should have a clear "view" of the room). The sink and refrigerator (with their watery, wintry symbolism) should stand at least two feet away from the stove (since it symbolizes fire). The best kitchens are symmetrical and shielded from the front door. The food preparation area should not be exposed on more than two sides. Separate food preparation "islands," though convenient, aren't good feng shui. The center of the kitchen should be clear and open to allow chi to circulate.

student experience

"Remodeling the kitchen was the best money I've ever spent. Prior to remodeling, the stove was directly in line with the front door of the house, and all of the appliances were right on top of each other. Once the stove and other appliances were placed more appropriately, cooking and meal time became such a pleasure."
—Matt, management consultant

Make sure that the cook can stand in a comfortable position without having to turn his or her back to an entryway. A nervous cook can pass negative energy to the family.

Your kitchen should never be above or below a bathroom. You don't want anyone using the toilet directly above the place where the family meal is being cooked. Likewise, you don't want water draining away below your kitchen, taking with it all the prosperity you've "cooked up." Don't let your stove even "see" a toilet from its vantage point at the heart of your kitchen.

If you're going to spend serious money remodeling your home to amend its feng shui, the kitchen will most likely give you more return for your dollar than any other room. It's worth the investment to have a solid, safe, efficient, clean environment in which to nourish your family. Before you undertake any major feng shui remodeling project, it's wise to consult a certified feng shui consultant. See the Sources appendix in the back of this book for more details.

YOUR BEDROOM

Just as your front door symbolizes your home's mouth, the living room its heart, and the kitchen its stomach, your bedroom symbolizes your family's relationships—particularly that of the husband and wife. The bedroom is the most important room: it's the symbolic home of the harmony and well-being of the entire household. All bedrooms, whether they are the master bedroom, the children's rooms, or guest rooms, require careful consideration, because we're most vulnerable to the effects of negative chi when we're asleep. Psychologically speaking, when we sleep we're defenseless, so security is paramount here. Bad bedroom feng shui can cause sleep disturbances and related illnesses.

This is one of the few rooms where plants should not be abundant. Their energy is so yang that too many of them could interfere with your family's ability to sleep deeply. If you're trying to spark a little sexual fire in the master bedroom, decorate with reds, pinks, and fiery symbolism. Just don't overdo it, or you could spark arguments instead. Pink and red spectrum colors enhance marital harmony and affection, and if you're single, these colors may help guide a relationship to you. In general, balance restful yin with arousing, rejuvenating yang energies in the bedroom.

The placement of your bed is one of the most important factors in bedroom feng shui. The head of your bed should rest against a solid "tortoise" wall. Place your bed so that you can see the door clearly, but don't put the bed directly in line with the door.

In the bedroom more than in any other room, it's important to avoid the "poison arrows" of sharp corners (like the kind that protrude in an L-shaped room) or knifelike shapes (like those created by vertical blinds). It's especially imperative that corners don't aim their sha chi directly at the bed. Never place a bed under an exposed beam (this may cause headaches), or hang shelves or other heavy features over the bed. Don't place an aquarium, or any symbols of water, in the bedroom. Water's powerful yang energy is disturbing to our sleep. Take televisions and computers out of the bedroom where you can. If you can't remove them, cover them and don't leave them on when anyone is trying to sleep. Don't run power cords under the bed; their electromagnetic energy is especially harmful when you're sleeping.

If you simply can't change bad bedroom feng shui, do what you can to remedy it. If the bed must face a door, place a screen in front of it, but make sure that you hang a mirror that allows the person in the bed to see anyone entering the room. At the very least, suspend a crystal ball or wind chime between the bed and the doorway. Hang a soft, sheer fabric over exposed beams to shield sleepers from their oppressive energy. Place a plant between the bed and any window. Windows, as long as they're not so large that they dominate the room, are beneficial because they let in natural light, but they can also allow rushing chi to enter the room. The plant absorbs some of this energy, as do draperies, which should be closed when you're sleeping.

 a note from
the instructor

SEX ENHANCERS FOR THE BEDROOM

- Soft red or pink light
- Red bed sheets
- Scented candles
- Pair of mandarin duck or crane sculptures or images
- Peonies (for young couples only)

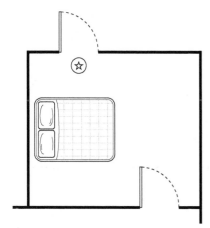

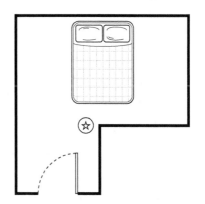

Problem:
Bedroom door leading
outside

Solution:
Keep door closed, and
hang a wind chime
above it ✪

Problem:
Corner protruding

Solution:
Hang crystal ball
at corner ✪

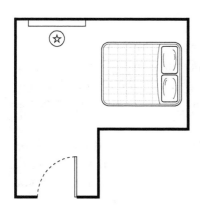

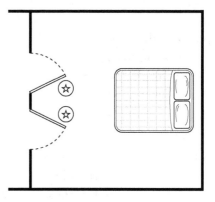

Problem:
Doorway is hidden from
the bed

Solution:
Place mirror to give sleepers
a view of the door ✪

Remedies for bad bedroom feng shui.

Problem:
2 doors clash in
bedroom

Solution:
Tie red ribbons on
knobs ✪

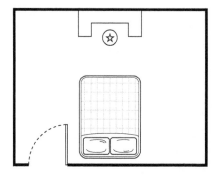
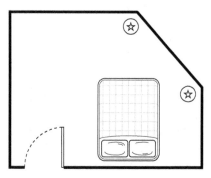

Problem:
Fireplace in bedroom

Solution:
Place plant in front
of fireplace ⊛

Problem:
Angled wall in bedroom

Solution:
Place plants or crystals
to soften angle ⊛

Remedies for bad bedroom feng shui.

KIDS' BEDROOMS

The feng shui of children's bedrooms can be tricky. Their rooms need to be full of yang to stimulate their growth and learning—and to complement their own natural high-yang energy—but they must also be rich in soothing yin energy to promote adequate rest and quiet concentration for young scholars. Kids' rooms with the best feng shui have areas devoted to each energy state: bright, yang play areas; secure, restful yin sleep areas.

Where should you locate your child's room? It's said that children who sleep in bedrooms in the front of the house develop a strong sense of independence. And of course, the right center of the ba-gua octagon, which belongs to children, is a natural place for children's rooms.

Invite your children to get involved in choosing and arranging their own décor. Encourage them to select light greens and blues for their walls and décor; these colors stimulate development and intelligence. Add a bit of metal for creativity. Help them choose friendly, loving images to display on their walls.

Children are extremely vulnerable to harmful chi, especially at night. Remove anything that might cause nightmares. Never decorate a child's room (not even a teenager's room) with threatening or violent images. If your child must play with "war" toys (military equipment, guns), encourage them to put these toys away out of sight at bedtime. Make sure no shelves, cupboards, or heavy pictures overhang the bed. Fill dark, foreboding corners with friendly, comforting objects, like favorite stuffed animals.

YOUR BATHROOMS

By their nature, bathrooms are challenging areas. Their strong water symbolism, their associations with dirt and waste, and the fact that we make ourselves vulnerable when we're in them make them dangerous places. In a bygone era, bathrooms were separate from the main living areas—often, they were in a detached building. But today, with the rise of modern plumbing, we're faced with the dilemma of where to put such a potentially inauspicious room, and how to minimize its potentially harmful effects.

The best bathrooms are away from other areas of the house. The toilet should have the protection of all four guardians: a strong tortoise wall at its back, and dragon and tiger guardians to either side. Toilet cubicles are ideal for this reason. The toilet should not be in a direct line with the door. Always remember to keep the toilet seat cover down.

Large windows are an added plus. Place lots of live plants in the bathroom to absorb moisture and enhance natural chi. Keep all bathrooms clean, clear, and bright; keep all plumbing and fixtures in good working order. Close the bathroom door before, during, and after use. A closed door won't block all of the inauspicious bathroom chi, but it does help to keep it "out of sight; out of mind."

RECREATION ROOMS

These casual rooms may be located in the less protected areas of your house, since their function is less vital than sleeping, cooking, and bathing areas. Fill them with comfortable, enlivening décor, and create areas the entire household can enjoy. Books are an excellent choice for this room, and a selection of art supplies, board games, and puzzles encourages positive, constructive play.

YOUR DINING ROOMS

The dining room is doubly important: It's the place where the family members (and their guests) gather to nourish themselves and to socialize. According to traditional Chinese culture, seating is an elaborate affair: Each seat carries its own status. The head of the household takes the command position (a clear view of the entire room and the entry, with its back against a solid "tortoise" wall)—unless an honored guest is expected at dinner, and then the command position is offered to the guest. Regardless of seating order, all diners should have a clear view of one another.

Dining tables should be round or oval, like the heaven they symbolize, though octagons, squares, and rectangles are acceptable—as long as nobody will be "pierced" by the sha chi of their corners. But avoid tables with "missing" corners. Always buy a dining table slightly larger than you need. If you'll regularly serve four, buy a table for six, and so on.

Dining rooms work best when decorated with food-related colors: soft pink, red, peach, or green. But if you want your diners to eat less, try decorating in black and white or blue—these colors suppress the appetite.

This room, like the kitchen, is rich in wealth and abundance symbolism. Enhance this connection by placing a large mirror on the wall where it will reflect (and thereby magnify) the scrumptious bounty on the table. Pictures of abundant ripe fruit and similar images also convey notions of plenty.

It's important to keep energies balanced in the dining room—too much yin or yang can create digestive problems. Above all, make sure no one sits with his or her back to a protruding corner or under exposed ceiling beams. If you have an upstairs bathroom positioned directly over the dining room, move it if at all possible. There could hardly be an unluckier symbol than having someone eliminating right over your head while you're eating.

If the dining room door is uncomfortably close to the table, hang curtains or crystal balls to keep diners from feeling as though they need to eat and run. If the dining room is small and cramped, add mirrors. Tradition has it that if you have an empty place at the table, leave the chair in place to close the circle.

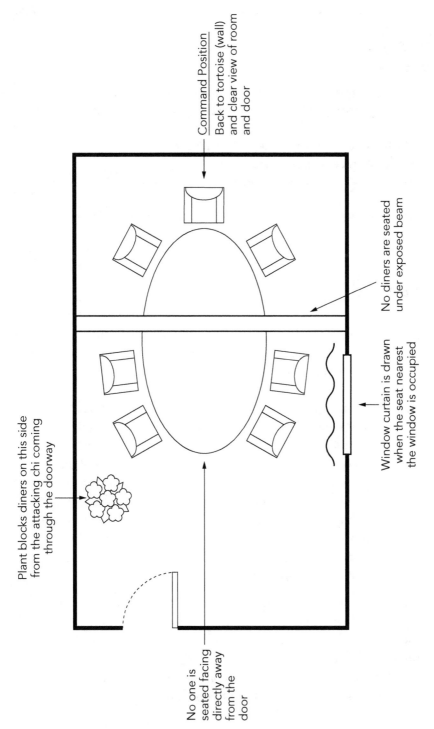

Command Position
Back to tortoise (wall) and clear view of room and door

No diners are seated under exposed beam

Window curtain is drawn when the seat nearest the window is occupied

Plant blocks diners on this side from the attacking chi coming through the doorway

No one is seated facing directly away from the door

Suggested dining room seating.

a note from
the instructor

DIETING? TRY THESE FENG SHUI APPETITE SUPPRESSANTS IN THE DINING ROOM

- Decorate the room in blue, or in black and white.
- Set the table with blue cloths and mats.
- Use small plates to make servings appear large, even if portions are small.
- Serve even humble food with elegance, suggesting wealth and plenty.

HALLWAYS AND STAIRS

The halls and stairs are the lungs and veins of your home, drawing chi throughout its interior. Just as your lungs and veins must be in good working order if you're going to stay healthy, your home's halls and stairs must be bright, clean, clutter free, and inviting.

Hallways: Hallways should be short, wide, airy, and full of cheery yang light. Avoid long hallways that force you to pass through more than three doorways. A hallway that leads directly from the front door to a back door is bad feng shui; it encourages entering chi to flow right back outside again. Deflect the chi's path with a curtain, plant, small table, statuary, wind chime, crystal ball, or fountain near the back door. Slow down the accelerating chi in a long hallway with the same devices: plants, lighting, and attractive décor will make the hall seem less tunnel-like.

Staircases: Chi rises and falls to other levels of your home primarily via staircases, so it's important that they be broad and well lit. But because flowing chi can accelerate on the slopes of staircases, they should never point directly toward your front door or toward a bedroom or bathroom. Good feng shui staircases curve gracefully to one side or the other, mimicking the flow of chi. Foil the attacking chi of straight staircases by placing plants at the bottom (to either side).

Avoid spiral staircases, as they can torque the chi into a chaotic funnel. Also avoid bi-level staircases like those in split-foyer houses—these may negatively influence the chi in the family. If your home has one of these, wrap a continuous green silk vine around the banisters of both stairways. If the steps of your stairway are open at the back, consider enclosing them—not only do open steps fail to provide the symbolic stability you need when you're climbing them, they also cause rising chi to spill over the edges and cascade back to ground level.

STORAGE ROOMS, BASEMENTS, ATTICS, AND GARAGES

Unfortunately, all of these areas can be a source of bad chi because of their associations with stagnation, bad smells, cleaning equipment, household items in need of repair, and clutter.

Storage rooms: Since these areas are less frequently used, they're ideally suited to parts of your home with less desirable chi. If you have a storage room with bad chi and you can't immediately do anything to fix it, keep it as quiet as you can so that the bad chi won't be stirred up. Don't place storage rooms directly above or below kitchens, dining rooms, or important bedrooms. Their emptiness and stagnation can affect diners and sleepers.

Basements: Make sure basements are dry. A damp, leaky basement is a severe hazard to beneficial chi. Keep basements clean, clear, and clutter-free. Light them well, and air them out frequently.

Attics: Don't give in to the temptation to overstuff your attic. A glut of unused possessions symbolizes stagnant chi, and a life that doesn't have room for new opportunities. Keep your attic ventilation in good working order to circulate any chi that might get trapped up there.

Garages: The best garages are detached from the house so that the rushing energy the cars bring with them will not transfer to the house. If the garage is attached, having a utility room or breezeway between it and the house can help diffuse this energy. Avoid having a bedroom over the garage if possible, where you're least protected at your most vulnerable times.

FENG SHUI LESSON-END QUESTIONS

Lesson #5:

1. With what areas of your home are you unsatisfied, and why?

_____

_____

_____

_____

_____

_____

2. What particular rooms or areas of your home leave you feeling drained, jangled, or depressed?

_____

_____

_____

_____

_____

_____

3. As you evaluate each area of your home, look for correlations between the state of the room and the state of your life; for instance, could the fact that your savings keep draining away be related to that leaky kitchen sink in your Wealth area? As these potential connections occur to you, write them down.

_____

_____

_____

_____

_____

_____

_____

Other Thoughts:

_____

_____

_____

_____

_____

_____

feng shui outdoors

Choosing and Improving Your Neighborhood • Four
Guardians for Your Home • Yard and Garden Feng Shui

FENG SHUI AND YOUR NEIGHBORHOOD

Traditional Chinese belief has it that the earth is a living being. Just as
different parts of our home symbolize different body parts, any given
portion of the earth has its own individual chi. Our home's location and
orientation to the earth (and by extension, to the entire universe) can
have a profound effect on our fortune.

Determining the feng shui of a given location has much to do with
common sense and intuition: Some places just make you feel more comfortable, secure, and energized than others. Areas with abundant natural beauty provide better living spaces than areas with clutter, decay,
and urban sprawl.

When determining an area's suitability, start by using your nose:
Does the air smell fresh and healthy? Can you catch the scent of green,

growing things on the breeze? If the air is stagnant in a given location, it will be difficult to keep up a healthy flow of chi. At the same time, you don't want to live in an area that's whipped frequently by a strong sha chi wind. A light, undulating breeze is ideal.

Next, survey the land around you. Chinese culture favors the presence of mountains and hills; it's said that these are the abode of dragons. It's great to have solid, protective hills around your home. Just avoid jagged, overwhelming mountains, and don't choose a home where your front door "confronts" a mountain. Also, never situate your house on the mountain's crest.

It's also a benefit to have water nearby, as long as it's clean and gently flowing. You don't want to be too near a straight channel of water. Living too close to the ocean is hazardous because it's difficult to balance the influence of that much water. It's beneficial to live inside the gentle "bow" of a river. Avoid living at the outside curve or the "Y" where two rivers converge.

A reasonably well-traveled road nearby is generally not a bad feature, particularly if it meanders casually, but you don't want to be too near a freeway or busy intersection because these places are hotbeds of fast and chaotic chi. On the other hand, you don't want to live on a dead-end street, because chi has nowhere to flow, and tends to get trapped and stagnate.

 a note from
the instructor

ARGUING NEIGHBORS? FOUR WAYS TO BLOCK THEIR SHA CHI

- Plant a row of healthy shrubs to absorb and diffuse negative chi.
- Put on headphones and tune the radio between stations so the "white noise" will block the sounds of the argument.
- Counter with your own upbeat, positive chi: sing, dance, play music, turn on lights, and radiate beneficial thoughts toward your arguing neighbors.
- Build a fence.

Bad: At the top of
a T-junctionn

Good: Inside the bend
of a gently flowing river

Bad: On a cul-de-sac

Good: Near (but not too near)
a briskly travelled (but not
too busy) road

Bad: Near a freeway
or railroad tracks

Good and bad house locations.

These days, of course, many of us are city dwellers, and we don't have the luxury of living in a verdant stretch of mountains or near natural bodies of water. But our surroundings still affect us in many of the same ways. Tall buildings act upon us as mountains and hills do, and roads may function as rivers. In general, if you're an urbanite, follow the same principles we just outlined but substitute human-made structures for natural landforms, and roads and streets for bodies of water.

Choose areas with lively energy—but not too much of it. Avoid living near places where the public gathers, such as airports, churches, schools, and sports arenas. The energy such places give off can often be negative and unsettling. In general, they generate too much yang chi.

For exactly the opposite reasons, you want to avoid living near places associated with illness, decay, and death, such as graveyards, funeral homes, landfills, animal shelters, and slaughterhouses. These places can infuse your home with dangerous yin "death" chi.

Neighborhoods with the best feng shui are full of happy families living in well-maintained homes. If your neighbors show signs of prosperity and good fortune, that's a pretty reliable indicator that the area is a lucky one. Choose a neighborhood like this from the start if you can, but if you're unable to move, deflect "bad vibes" from unhappy neighbors with wind chimes, walls, fences, and plants.

a note from
the instructor

FORM FENG SHUI

Form feng shui, the study of the flow of chi through a given landscape, is the oldest school of feng shui. This school makes extensive use of the four landform guardians: the black tortoise, the red bird, the green dragon, and the white tiger. It also looks for the presence of the five elements, and pays close attention to the movement of water and wind in a given location. Form feng shui has been used since ancient times to choose gravesites, as well as business and home locations. For more information on the Form school, see Lesson 1 and the resources in Appendix A.

The Five Elements in Your Neighborhood

The five elements are present, to varying degrees, in the landscape of any given location. The ideal location contains a harmonious balance of all five elements, but it's nearly impossible to find such a place. The more balanced the elements in a given location, the better its feng shui, but certain personality types benefit most from the presence of specific elements (we'll discuss personality in greater detail in Lesson 11). To find the elements in your neighborhood, look for the following shapes in the land and buildings around your home:

Fire: Fire landforms are pointy and triangular. Look for craggy mountains or buildings with triangular features. A neighborhood where these landforms and structures are abundant will benefit you if you're an earth person, but will exhaust and fatigue you if you're a wood or metal person.

Earth: Earth mountains and hills are rectangular and flat-topped. Earth buildings are flat and low, and convey an aura of solidness. Nearly everyone benefits from having earth landforms and structures around, except water people. For a highly temperamental metal person, a little earthiness in his or her surroundings is almost a necessity.

Metal: The domed humps of metal mountains symbolize mounds of gold stored up for you. Metal landforms benefit everyone except wood people.

Water: A verdant series of undulating mountain peaks, forming a dragon shape, are especially good for attracting luck and money. Even a wavy stand of lush trees can make a suitable water landform. This is the natural domain of water people, but fire people won't be comfortable here.

Wood: Tall, conical mountains with rounded tops and greenish hues are seldom seen in North America, but their equivalent is sometimes found, for example, in skyscrapers, and in graceful old farm silos. Wood landforms and structures nourish wood and fire personalities, but earth people will feel intruded upon.

Fire

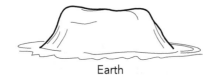

Earth

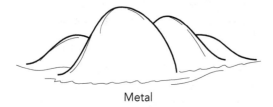

Metal

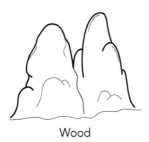

Wood

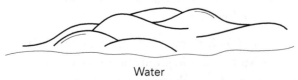

Water

Elemental landforms.

YOUR HOME'S FOUR GUARDIANS

Form feng shui, the oldest feng shui school, recommends that you choose a home that is protected from harmful forces by the four mythological Chinese guardians: the black tortoise, the green dragon, the white tiger, and the red bird. Various features in the landscape around your home represent these powerful beings, each with its own symbolic duty.

The Black Tortoise

In traditional Chinese culture, the long-lived tortoise is synonymous with longevity. It's also a potent symbol of protection, associated with heroes in Chinese folklore and mythology. Another term for the grim, armor-plated tortoise is "dark warrior," although, interestingly enough, it is always seen as a female creature.

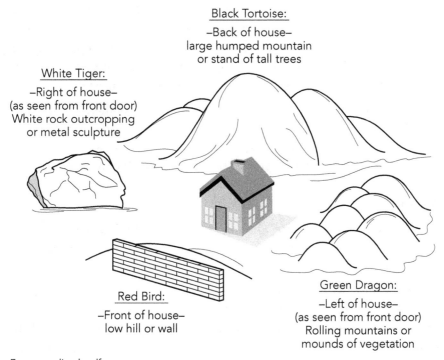

Four guardian landforms.

Your tortoise guardian stands watch at the back of your home, guarding it from perils and shielding it from the piercing cold of winter. The tortoise is the most powerful of your four guardians—and the one you least want to be without. Even if your home is missing all three of its other guardians, make sure it has a good tortoise at its back.

If you lack a tortoise, you may find yourself without adequate support. Friends and family may not stand with you in times of crisis; business associates may betray you when you need them most.

Your black tortoise can be a tall hill, a grove of trees, or a tall (but not oppressive) building. A grand old barn makes a good "artificial" tortoise. But to be an effective guardian, it must be taller than your home. If you have no tortoise, create one by planting a grove of trees.

The Green Dragon

Chinese culture is replete with dragons, the mythical conveyors of fortune. Dragons symbolize your ability to attract good luck and prosperity. Green dragons are particularly potent, because they're associated with the wood element, and with vibrant, growing chi. Without a proper green dragon drawing luck your way, you may find that you're missing opportunities in life and that your finances are not flourishing as you'd hoped.

Find your dragon to the left of your home as you stand looking out your front door. The best green dragons in nature are long lines of gently undulating hills, mountains, or forests. If you're missing a dragon, plant a row of fluffy bushes: yews, arbor vitaes, and boxwoods work well.

The White Tiger

In Chinese culture, the rare white tiger carries a mythical status. Unlike the ordinary orange tiger (an extremely yang creature), white tigers are considered yin.

The white tiger represents vigilance. Whereas the green dragon helps to bring you wealth and good fortune, the white tiger protects what you have and keeps it from slipping away or going bad. An ancient Chinese proverb states that the tiger is yang while awake and yin while asleep; think, then, of your white tiger as a potent sentry resting atop your wealth, sleeping with one eye open. The white tiger may not look very dangerous until aroused—then watch out!

If you want to hang on to what's good in your life, you need a sturdy white tiger. Without a proper tiger, your investments may go sour, your relationships might falter, and your successes may be short lived.

Find your white tiger guardian to the right of your home as you look out your front door. Natural white tigers are pale outcroppings of rock or other whitish landforms. A strong pale building can also serve as a white tiger. If you have no tiger, place a white stone to the right of your home. A pale metal sculpture works well too, because the tiger's element is metal.

The Red Bird

The red bird is associated with the sun and all things southern. It's sometimes called the red phoenix, although it's not associated with the mythological phoenix in any other way.

Located at the front of your home, your red bird serves as a gentle buffer between your home and the outside world. It's an excellent foil for attacking and rushing chi from busy streets.

The ideal red bird is a small hill or wall, lower than your home, with an open stretch in front of it. Good feng shui states that chi should have a *ming tang*, or "bright hall"—literally, a gathering space in which to collect before it enters your home.

If you don't have a good red bird, you can create one by installing a low brick wall or low redwood fence. Be careful not to build it too high, because it could block good fortune from entering. Keep your ming tang clean, clear, and well maintained.

It's best to have all four guardians around your home, whether they are in natural or human-made form. But what if you live in an apartment? Suppose you can't find your guardians in the surrounding environment, and can't do anything to modify your home's exterior?

That's where symbolism comes in. When all else fails, place figures and images of the four guardians as near as possible to their corresponding areas. Most Chinese import shops and feng shui stores will sell some form of these guardians. Also, decorate those areas with the colors and elements native to each guardian: black/water for your tortoise, green/wood for your dragon, white/metal for your tiger, and red/fire for your bird.

a note from
the instructor

YOUR FOUR GUARDIANS: THEIR POSITIONS, DUTIES, ELEMENTS, AND COLORS

GUARDIAN	GUARDS WHAT	POSITION	ELEMENT	COLORS
Tortoise	Household	Rear	Water	Black, Blue
Dragon	Income Potential	Left	Wood	Green
Tiger	Protection	Right	Metal	White
Bird	Opportunities	Front	Fire	Red

YOUR LOT'S FENG SHUI

The shape of your home's lot affects the amount and quality of chi that reaches your house. The areas of the ba-gua octagon play out on your lot in much the same way that they do inside, so it's important to have all areas well represented.

The best lots are symmetrical: either squares or rectangles. It's beneficial to have a lot that is slightly narrower at the front than at the back: the lot will "hold on" to the good chi it accumulates. Unfortunately, the reverse also holds true: a lot that is wider at the front has difficulty holding on to good chi. The worst lot shapes are triangles (these can be disastrous) and L- or T-shaped lots with "missing" corners.

If you have a less-than-ideal lot shape, you can perform a number of adjustments to minimize the harmful effects. Adjust an irregular lot by planting bushes along its offending side. Place outdoor lights or flagpoles in tight corners and constricting spaces. Aim a bright floodlight from the edge of missing areas toward the center of the house.

Your house should sit as close to the center of your lot as possible. If it sits too close to the front, you may need to add a water feature or low wall to buffer the large amounts of chi reaching you from the outside world. If it's situated too close to the back, you'll need a wide, well-lit pathway to conduct the chi to your house. Plant more greenery in the front to balance the lot.

Missing corner:

Place light, flag, or statue

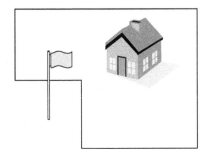

Lot with odd angle:

Plant trees along the odd line, or fill corner with landscaping, statuary, or lighting

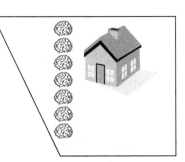

House close to front lot:

Light home and back of lot; place shrubs, trees, flags, pinwheels, or low wall as a buffer between home and outside lot

Sloping lot:

Light the home; light driveway leading to the home

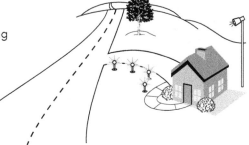

Improving the lot your home is on.

a note from
the instructor

FU DOGS: LOYAL ENTRY GUARDIANS

If you've ever visited China, you've seen them: pairs of fierce, pug-faced, lion-like stone creatures flanking driveways and walks. These are fu dogs, mythical guardians of Chinese homes since ancient times, and are still popular across Asia today.

Fu dogs, like their non-stone, living brethren, happily guard the household from negative influences even when their owners are away. Just as with real canines, size doesn't matter: even small fu dogs can get the job done—although in general, the size of your dogs should match the size of your home.

Find a pair of fu dogs in nearly any fine statuary shop and in Chinese import stores. Place your dogs on pedestals so that they can "see" better, and light them up at night.

Fu dogs.

The slope of your lot affects the way chi reaches your home. Your house should rest on a symmetrical plot of level or gently upward-sloping land. If your home is on a downward slope, light the front of the house and all the drives and walks leading to it, and plant bushes to act as buffers against the swift-moving chi flowing downhill toward your home.

Your driveway should not point directly at the house. If at all possible, it should curve or meander slightly, the way chi does. Your driveway should be spacious and inviting. A narrow driveway limits opportunities. A forked drive encourages quarrels within the family. The best driveways are made of natural materials that harmonize with the local landscape.

Any steps leading to your home should be broad, low, and well lit.

YARD AND GARDEN FENG SHUI

A yard with good feng shui continues the same symbolism and principles at work inside. Trees and shrubs nurture beneficial chi and buffer the home from harsh outside influences. A well-planned garden can enhance the areas of the ba-gua octagon just as the inside of the home does.

Trees are generally auspicious as long as they're healthy and properly pruned. They can fill in missing corners of a lot, and are particularly helpful when they flank a driveway like sentries. If you're missing a tiger or dragon guardian, trees that embody their qualities can fill in for them. Fruit trees are especially lucky. If you live in a seasonal climate, keep them in pots and bring them inside during winter months.

 a note from
the instructor

LUCKY FLOWERS, PLANTS, AND TREES

Flowers: Lotus, peony, orchid
Plants: Jade, bamboo, philodendron
Trees: Fruit trees, magnolia, pine

Bright, healthy flowers, almost always yang, add a cheery presence to your yard. Use their colors in the same way you use colors symbolically indoors: yellows for earth, reds for fire, blues for water, and so forth. Plan a perennial garden so that something is coming into bloom just as the previous blooms are fading. Choose flowers that do well when cut, and you'll have a source of fresh décor for the inside of your home as well.

But don't feel that you need to limit yourself to trees and flowers. Sculptures, statuary, even stones and pebbles can enhance the feng shui of your yard and garden. The presence of a few stone and metal pieces help you keep abundant wood and water energies balanced. Lanterns, path lights, candles, fire rings, and even barbecues can lend a fiery yang essence to your garden.

Ponds and other water features in your backyard get mixed reviews from feng shui experts. For the most part they're beneficial—as long as they're not too large in proportion to the house, and the water inside them flows toward the home. But a large amount of water, particularly if it's close to your home, can pose a threat to the household. Backyard swimming pools have a dubious reputation for this reason: it's risky to have a large quantity of water pooling at your back. A modest-sized pool, particularly if it's round or oval and spaced well apart from the house, is unlikely to cause harm.

Structures standing in the yard and garden are generally considered auspicious, particularly if their design harmonizes with the house. Gazebos, Jacuzzis, birdbaths, and other lawn ornaments are a plus. Trellises, porches, and gardens are all good buffers against the unpredictable outside world.

 a note from
the instructor

PLANTS AND TREES TO AVOID

Cactus: Their prickly spines generate poison arrows.
Willows: Any drooping plants that look "depressed" might encourage their owners to share their mood!

a note from
the instructor

BA-GUA COLORS IN THE GARDEN

Re-create the ba-gua in the colors you use for corresponding sectors of your garden. Select the appropriate colors of your favorite varieties, or plant the following:

Career (bottom center)—Black: black pansies and lilies, black-eyed Susans

Knowledge (bottom left)—Blue: bluebells, hydrangeas, morning glories

Family (left)—Green: ferns, dill, parsley, liriope, shamrocks

Wealth (top left)—Purple: lavender, heather, larkspur, aster, rhododendron

Fame (top center)—Red: roses, salvia, poppies

Marriage (top right)—Pink: Sweet William, vinca

Children (right)—White: moonflowers, alyssum, lilies of the valley

Helpful People (bottom right)—Gray: dusty miller, artemisia, thyme, rosemary

Health (center)—Yellow/Russet: daylilies, marigolds, daffodils

If you live in an apartment or townhouse, don't despair. You can still avail yourself of beneficial garden energies. A townhouse patio or balcony can be enhanced beautifully with potted plants and hanging baskets—and even here, you can balance ba-gua energies. But if your closest contact with the outdoors is a window (which I hope, at least, you can open), bring the benefits of garden energies into your home with colorful window boxes. Don't bother trying to re-create the ba-gua on this small a scale; just cultivate as much vibrant, cheery plant life as you can.

BRINGING IT ALL TOGETHER

Now that we've explored the feng shui of outdoor areas, let's put it all together. First we'll look at a plan for evaluating an area you're thinking of living in, and then we'll discuss ways you can improve your neighborhood's feng shui if you're unable, or unwilling, to move.

But Is It Home?

When you're searching for a new home, take a walking tour of the neighborhood if at all possible. It's important to get out there and immerse yourself in the environment for an extended period of time.

Reach out with your senses, and trust them. Does this area relax you, or make you feel tenser? Do you feel a sense of trust and peace, or do you feel a nagging uneasiness? It's best to take this walk on a day when you're relaxed, calm, and rested to begin with so that you can gather the most reliable information.

If your potential new neighborhood passes this initial "feel" test, get the rest of your senses in on the experiment. Breathe in the air, look around you, and listen. Even in the city, it's possible to find tree-lined neighborhoods that exude a quiet, natural order: This is the place you're looking for. Also observe the state of the properties around you, and the cars parked outside: How well maintained are they? Does the area look as though it's accustomed to a steady stream of good fortune, or does it appear to be in decline? Do you get a sense of peace, happiness, and prosperity, particularly from your nearest neighbors?

If you really want to make sure you're moving into an area with a good pattern of luck, do some research: Check the recent history of the area, and especially that of the property you're buying. Any tragedies or disasters? How about foreclosures, or illnesses?

If this area still seems like the place for you, take a closer look at your new home's immediate surroundings: Can you identify your home's four guardians in nearby landforms and structures? If they're not in place already, can you envision a way to build them? Check the area for any obvious negatives, like jagged, harsh structures (barbed wire fences, electrical transformers, buildings with sharp protrusions), graveyards, military installations, hospitals, and so forth.

Finally, identify the dominant elements at work in your environment, and determine if they're what you need most. Does the area provide enough of the elements you need to sustain you? (See Lesson 11 on personalities for more details on the way each element nurtures various personalities.) If it doesn't, will you be able to introduce them? For instance, if you need wood, can you plant a substantial garden? If you need water, can you add a small pond?

Attracting Better Chi to a Flawed Location

Let us reiterate that no place on Earth has utterly perfect feng shui, but every place can be improved. If you're happy with your current location in most respects, or for other reasons are unable or unwilling to move, you can take steps to improve your neighborhood's chi.

Let's assume that your neighborhood failed every aspect of the test in the previous section: It's rundown, cluttered, and befouled. There's nothing green for miles, except for whatever is oozing out of the drains at the slaughterhouse up the road. The neighbors argue constantly. Your home is overshadowed on both sides by dark, oppressive modern office buildings. But if you're still determined to live here, what steps can you take to carve an oasis of good chi out of this nightmare?

If possible, build a sturdy, tasteful fence or wall along the back of your property to provide you with a strong tortoise. Continue the wall along the property line that you share with your quarreling neighbors. Line this wall with fast-growing trees and shrubs to create a buffer of vibrant, growing chi. Plant fluffy trees to block out the view of those two tall buildings. Where you can't adequately block out negative elements, like the arguing neighbors or the ugly buildings, place small mirrors on the outside of your house to deflect the negative chi.

Next, do what you can to create a garden-like atmosphere in your immediate surroundings. Choose fragrant landscaping, like pine, eucalyptus, and rosemary, to help fill the air with natural scent. Add at least one water feature to help get the good chi flowing.

Finally, have parties: Invite everyone you know who is a source of positive, uplifting chi to come and visit you. Whenever people with good chi visit, they infuse their surroundings with their positive energy. In the scenario we've created here, you have a lot to work against, but if you're determined, you could be the one force that turns the area's misfortune around.

FENG SHUI LESSON-END QUESTIONS

Lesson #6:

1. How would you characterize the chi of your neighborhood?

_____

_____

_____

_____

_____

2. Which of the five elements are strongest in your neighborhood?

_____

_____

_____

_____

_____

3. Which of the five elements are weakest in your neighborhood?

_____

_____

_____

_____

_____

4. Does your home have all four guardians present in the surrounding landscape or structures? If not, list any ideas you have for ways to create your missing guardians.

_____

_____

_____

_____

5. How is your lot's Feng Shui? What aspects of shape or orientation need improvement? What ideas do you have for improving them?

_____

_____

_____

_____

Other Thoughts:

_____

_____

_____

_____

_____

_____

feng shui for your workplace and career

Feng Shui at the Office • Home Offices, Studios, and Workshops • How Feng Shui Can Aid Your Career

To many Chinese businesspeople, feng shui is an essential part of doing business. American corporations setting up headquarters where large numbers of employees are Chinese have quickly learned the importance of investing in a feng shui expert's services. As well they should: Feng shui has been enhancing businesses for thousands of years!

Good business feng shui boosts your power to compete, heightens security, and strengthens finances. If you're a business owner, good feng shui is synonymous with prosperity: It gives you and your employees a mental and emotional "leg up," which, though subtle, can spell real success. If you're an employee, it can help you enhance your career every step of the way.

Each of the five elements is conducive to certain business activities, as well as particular types of businesses. Most businesses tap each of the five elements at one time or another (even a heavily "water"-related business like a railroad or shipping company avails itself of earth energies when it hosts a company picnic). Follow the same rules of décor and symbolism we've discussed throughout the book by adding symbols of the appropriate element and its support element to enrich a particular activity, and avoiding symbols of the corresponding "damaging" element.

Here is a list of careers grouped according to their dominant element:

Wood (growth, kindness, persistence): Teaching, religious vocations, businesses related to lumber and furniture, grocery-related businesses, textiles, writing and publishing, law, seasonal and cyclical business (such as fashion)

Fire (emotional expression, generosity): Food service, fuel-related industries, heating and lighting, anything to do with firearms, glass-blowing, computer repair, performing arts, sales and promotion, public speaking, industries that involve radiation and lasers

Earth (stability, trust): Farming, ecology, law, construction, human resources, accounting, real estate, brokerage firms, insurance, consultation, funeral services

Water (wisdom, love, freedom): Transportation, communication, tourism, teaching, journalism, public speaking, laundry services, fishing, medical fields, music

Metal (precision, planning, aesthetics, righteousness): Event planning, engineering, promotion, automotive fields, jeweler, industries involving machinery and metalworking

HOW TO SURVIVE EIGHT HOURS A DAY AT THE OFFICE

As we've discussed, feng shui recognizes our need for nature; it strives to bring more of the natural world into our "unnatural" indoor existence. Unfortunately, there's hardly a more unnatural place than an office building—and many of us are stuck in such a place for more than half our waking hours!

Feng shui can help mediate some of the stress and damage caused by the chaotic harshness of an office environment. But the best way to minimize the threat an office poses to your personal chi is to get out of there whenever you can! Take walks outside on your breaks. Eat your lunch someplace other than where you work, if at all possible. Practice yoga and other stress-relieving rituals. Exercise and rest regularly, and eat an excellent diet. Take regular days off, and limit your weekly work hours to a sensible number. Remember, feng shui is the art of balance. You will not succeed in business by neglecting other aspects of your life.

Now let's take a look at what you can do to make the time you must spend at the office as healthful and auspicious as possible.

CHOOSING YOUR OFFICE

The best office locations in a given building or suite are not directly in line with the doorway or street. Try to choose an office that opens onto a clear, inviting space—your ming tang.

 a note from
the instructor

DOS AND DON'TS OF DESK PLACEMENT

Do:

- Place your desk so that you're facing the door.
- Place your desk so that you can see the door when you work at your computer.
- Place your desk so that you sit with your back to a solid wall.
- Place your desk where you have a maximum view of everyone else present.
- Place your desk so there are more objects in front of you than behind you.

Don't:

- Place your desk directly in front of a door or window. Especially, don't place it so that your back is to a window.
- Place your desk in a cramped corner.
- Place your desk so near the front door that you become distracted.
- Place your desk so that it "confronts" a boss or coworker.

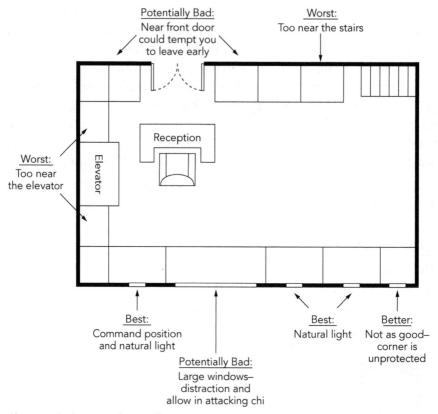

Choosing the location of your office.

If you're in an open office, avoid choosing a desk too near the exit, or you'll be plagued with thoughts of leaving work early. By all means, avoid a desk that is close to an elevator or stairwell; you don't want that kind of chaotic chi nearby. Avoid choosing an office with too many windows, or you'll find yourself drawn to the view outside instead of to your work.

The best offices are toward the back of the suite but easily accessible. They should be well lit. Above all, they must be in good repair and clutter free.

ENHANCING AN EXISTING OFFICE

Place your desk in the command position, or as close to it as you can. This means that you're facing the door so that you can see anyone who enters but you're not sitting directly in line with it. Do what you can to assure that you have a strong tortoise at your back. Don't sit with your back to a window, doorway, or interior glass wall.

Even a partition is better than no tortoise, but a solid wall is best. In general, you'll be more productive if there is more (of everything) in front of you than behind you—this gives you the subconscious impression of opportunities before you. Set up your computer so that you're still facing the door when you're working at it.

If the room is too small, you can place a mirror to make the area feel more spacious. If there's nothing you can do to change the position of your desk, and you can't see the doorway from where you're sitting, place a mirror where it will give you a view of the door.

It's imperative to avoid "poison arrows" at work. Cover or muffle any protruding corners (90-degree angles created by filing cabinets and so forth) in your workspace—there tend to be lots of them in offices. Where you can, drape soft fabric over them, hang wind chimes and crystal balls, or place potted plants in front of them.

Watch out for "dead" spaces: corners and niches, where chi may stagnate. Place something cheery in these spaces, such as a plant, a lamp, or a bright painting.

But what if your office is in a cubicle? These often-drab, dehumanizing, maze-like structures create some of the worst workplace feng shui. But even here, you can greatly improve the chi in your cubicle with a few simple steps.

Try to position your workspace in the cubicle so that you have a clear view of its entrance. If you have to sit with your back to the cubicle's opening, hang a mirror that allows you to see the entry.

Use plenty of plants with round, soft leaves to bring vibrant natural energy to your space. If you can't have real plants, silk ones are better than nothing, but avoid dried flowers, since they're essentially lifeless. A small tabletop water feature will bring soothing natural sound to your cubicle.

Office cubicles are almost always saturated with fluorescent lights, which can be jangling and fatiguing. You probably won't be able to turn them off, but you may be able to counteract some of their harmful effects by installing full-spectrum lighting.

It's unlikely that you'll be permitted to paint your cubicle, but you may be able to introduce some energizing color to it by covering your bulletin board and desk blotter with colorful fabric, and draping an afghan over your chair.

Finally, try to avoid working in an area of your cubicle that's overhung with cabinetry or shelving. Raise low-hung units where you can; where it's not possible to move them or reposition yourself, hang a crystal ball to diffuse the negative chi of their sharp corners and oppressive weight.

Good Office Arrangements

If you have a choice of desks, go for an oval, circle, or semicircle, especially if you're in a creative field: Organic shapes are the best all-purpose good-chi-attractors. Wood feeds creativity. Square and rectangular desks are stable, and good for attracting wealth.

Choose lighter colors for your desk: the darker your desktop, the harder you'll find it is to get anything done.

Decorate your office with symbols of luck and wealth: bright reds, purples, and greens. A small tabletop fountain creates the sensation of success trickling toward you. The only possessions that belong in your office are things that either help you get your job done or inspire you to do it better. Don't muddy your focus with pictures of hobbies or vacation destinations—unless you're a hobby shop owner or a travel agent!

The Ba-Gua in Your Office

Keep the ba-gua in mind as you arrange your workspace. The meanings that the ba-gua carries when applied to your home take on additional significance when you use them at work. At home, for example, your Children area may literally refer to your *children*. At work, it refers to your "creative children": your ideas, brainstorms, innovations, and projects. Similarly, your Marriage/Relationships area refers to the relationships you have with the pivotal people with whom you do business. Your Family area at work has more to do with the wider "family" of the community your business serves.

To make your workspace as auspicious as possible, arrange your work areas with the ba-gua in mind. Devote a portion of your Children area to keeping anything related to projects in development, since this area is rich in creative energies. Place organizers, calendars, and planners as close to the center of your workspace as you can—they're central to the health of your career. Store reference books and similar materials in your Knowledge area. Place your phone, Rolodex, and address book in Helpful People (these items represent your contacts to these people). Display symbols of your success (awards, trophies, diplomas, framed newspaper articles) in your Fame area.

The rules that apply to the ba-gua at home apply as well to the ba-gua at work. The same areas are associated with the same elements, and can be controlled or nourished by the presence of other elements and their symbols. Here, as at home, be aware of your symbolism; don't allow elemental symbols to clash. For example, avoid excess water symbolism in your Fame area (the domain of fire). Don't keep a fishbowl in the rear portion of your workspace; you don't want to "douse" (or even "dampen") the flame that's "heating up" your career. But you can attain great results by placing lights, triangular shapes, and red hues in this area, perhaps along with a little wood and wood symbolism (a plant, or wallpaper with vertical stripes) to support the fire element.

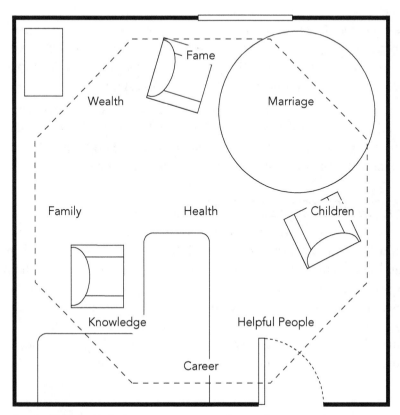

A typical office with the ba-gua octagon superimposed.

ENHANCING YOUR HOME OFFICE

If you work out of a home office, it's good feng shui to differentiate your workspace from your living space as much as possible. Keep work and sleep areas separate—if you must have an office in the bedroom, make it the "foldaway" kind, inside a closet or armoire, so that when the workday is done the office "vanishes." Take the same approach if your office area has to be in a room devoted to family gatherings.

It's as important to keep home life out of workspaces as it is to keep work out of home life. Treat your office door as though it's a front door. Place a sign with your name and profession on the door, your company logo, or a symbol of your profession, on the door. This will further differentiate it from the non-business areas of the house. Keep only work-related objects in your office.

Where should you locate your home office? This is a somewhat different issue than choosing an office in a crowded business suite, because you have more control over most aspects of the space, and there's generally far less human traffic to navigate. The front of your home is considered more yang and public; the back is more yin and private. Locate your office close to the front of your home if clients and customers will be visiting your office. Position it close to the back of the house if your business requires concentration and quiet.

If you work alone in isolation, bring a little stimulating movement and sound into your workspace. A ticking clock or water feature adds rhythmic, invigorating sound. Fish or other small, lively (but quiet) pets add an element of motion without creating too much of a distraction.

ENHANCING YOUR STUDIO OR WORKSHOP

Areas where creative work takes place must be extremely functional: clean, well lit, superbly organized, and clutter free. But they must also ignite and feed your creative energies. Include colors and images that inspire you and stir your creative juices. Since yang energy tends to flow upward, focus some of the lighting toward the ceiling to encourage rising yang energy. This is a great way to uplift the mood of an overly yin studio. But if too much yang is the problem, you may want to reduce the amount of up-lighting and focus more on muted lamps.

a note from
the instructor

CREATIVITY BOOSTERS FOR YOUR STUDIO OR WORKSHOP

- Keep your studio organized and clutter free.
- Decorate with fiery reds to "ignite" motivation.
- Accent with vibrant greens to help your ideas grow.
- Add judicious touches of metal, creativity's element.
- Place images and symbols that remind you of the kind of work and success you're striving for.
- Fill your space with sights, sounds, and scents that stimulate your creativity.

THE FENG SHUI OF BOSSES

If you're the boss of your company, it's especially important to get your business's feng shui right. It's imperative that your office has a solid tortoise, because a lot of negative things can happen behind your back. Managers who work with their backs to their employees often find they're the victims of gossip, backstabbing, and betrayal.

But don't go to the opposite extreme, either: Don't arrange your workers' cubicles in rows, and then sit at the front like a schoolteacher. This arrangement forces you to "confront" all your workers, and the work environment will turn testy and hostile.

THE FENG SHUI OF BUSINESS MEETINGS

The most auspicious arrangement for a business meeting is a large circular table—imagine King Arthur. But even the Round Table had a special place for the "throne." The leader of the meeting sits at the place that has the best tortoise and the best view of the door and all who enter. The nice thing about this arrangement is that it makes clear to all that the event has a leader but that everyone present is valued and has a voice. This is an especially good configuration for creative meetings and brainstorming sessions.

Avoid, if possible, the traditional type of "board meeting" arrangement that places people down two sides of a long, narrow table. Nearly everyone present is forced into "confrontation" mode, rarely an appropriate stance for productive business meetings. If you must sit at one of these tables, avoid sitting in a direct line to the door. Keep a good tortoise at your back, and sit at least one seat away from any corner.

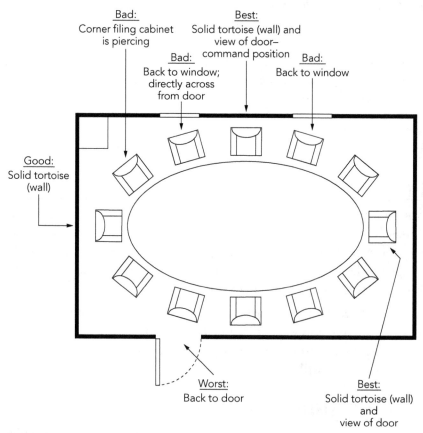

Best and worst seats in a meeting room.

a note from
the instructor

BUSINESS MEETINGS: BEST AND WORST SEATS

The Best Seats Give You:

- A clear view of the door
- A clear view of everyone present
- The greatest space between you and the door
- A solid tortoise at your back
- Trusted coworkers seated to your left and right (dragon and tiger)

The Worst Seats Place You:

- Directly in line with a door or window
- With your back to the door
- In a confrontational position with (directly across from) associates
- In an isolated corner
- With a table corner pointed directly at you

FENG SHUI AND YOUR CAREER

Feng shui can help you pave the way for career opportunities and foster attitudes of success. This is one of the easiest and most rewarding ways to use feng shui, and it's one of the primary ways it's used around the world. Done properly, feng shui can produce astonishing results.

But keep in mind that feng shui is not going to bring you instant fame and fortune. As with any endeavor, your feng shui enhancements are only as good as your attitude and must be coupled with sensible action.

For example, if you're courting a promotion, it's not enough to tie a string of Chinese coins to your appointment book (although this can be an extremely effective *enhancement*). You must also turn in a stellar job performance and maintain a positive, professional attitude. Do your part, and your feng shui efforts will complement them nicely.

student
experience

"I met Meihwa a few years ago at a seminar. I explained that my business was always 'just on the cusp' of getting contracts but never quite reaching them. I felt I was always short of capturing the contract or the sale. Meihwa asked me some questions about my business and where it was located. At the time, I was operating out of my basement. Meihwa suggested that I move my office from the basement to a much more prominent location on the second floor. I followed her instructions, and within a short time I secured a large contract.

"Over the years I have listened to everything Meihwa suggested. Her suggestions have brought me much success and abundance. I feel that I am blessed to have met Meihwa."

—Lisa, real estate agent

Remember that you have to start with the right intentions— the universe is far more likely to grant you recognition and success in your business endeavors if you honestly intend to perform a beneficial service. If you're greedy or power hungry, or you're after that promotion for the wrong reasons, feng shui is unlikely to help you—especially in the long run.

Remember that feng shui is deeply connected to Taoism, which states that what you put out into the universe will come back to you. Put forth what you hope to receive, and treat your superiors, inferiors, and colleagues as you wish to be treated. Be the kind of employee you'd want to promote if *you* were your boss!

Feng shui can't help you get ahead unfairly, but it *can* help you receive the recognition you deserve for your sincere efforts and hard work. It can also help you develop your social and communication skills; assist you in accumulating (appropriate) status and power; and help you rally mentors, assistants, colleagues, and helpful coworkers to your side. Couple right intentions with right actions, then add feng shui, and you've got a winning combination.

Feng shui can also help you determine the best careers to pursue, based on your astrology. In upcoming lessons, we'll identify your birth element and examine the careers that may make a good fit for your element. But for now, let's focus on enhancing your success in the career you're currently pursuing.

Career feng shui is different from wealth feng shui, although success in one generally brings success in the other. But where wealth feng shui focuses on the accumulation of money and material goods, career feng shui centers on your ability to gain power, influence, and fame within your field. It can help you avoid getting stuck in a rut or locked into a downward spiral. It can also help you get noticed and rise quickly through the ranks.

Choosing a Business Logo with Good Feng Shui

The logo, symbol, or emblem you choose to represent your company to the world can have a profound effect on its success. For example, many feng shui masters point to the lopsided, haphazard-looking "E" of Enron's logo as a portent of its financial disaster.

Good:
Lucky animal (Dragon)

Bad:
Jagged, unstable, and unbalanced

Good:
Healthy, well-rooted tree;
balanced image

Bad:
Ship (bearing wealth?)
is sailing <u>away</u> from your company

Good and bad business logos.

How do you select a logo that will bring success to your business and help deflect misfortune? As a general rule, choose balanced-looking shapes with a solid base if your company needs to project an air of stability (banking, investments, and the like). If your company deals in transportation, communication, or a similar industry, a graceful sweep to the logo, suggesting motion, may be favorable.

In general, stick with bright, lucky colors: reds, greens, blues, and yellows. Avoid dark, foreboding colors, or "weird" hues.

It's generally a good thing to choose a dragon, a horse, or any other traditionally lucky animal for your logo. If your company name appears alongside your chosen animal, just make sure it's placed near the animal's head, not its rear. It's never a good idea to position yourself too close to the rear of an animal.

FENG SHUI WORK HABITS

Keep beneficial chi flowing through areas devoted to your career by banishing clutter. Remember, clutter, dust, and dirt trap and repel vibrant, flowing chi. If your work area is dirty and disorganized, your career may suffer from a lack of healthy chi flow. In fact, if your career is not moving as swiftly as you'd like, take a long, hard look at the condition of your workspace. If it's piled high with folders you haven't touched in a month, if you can't lay hands on a pen without a rigorous search, and if you can't see your computer screen clearly through all the dust, you're probably looking straight at the culprit.

Good chi loves cleanliness and organization. Getting organized will not only improve the chi around you, it will also benefit your own personal chi. Organization reduces stress and permits you to focus more clearly on the task at hand. Then, of course, there are the practical benefits: you'll work more effectively (which never hurts your career), and you'll make a better impression.

Schedule the time to reorganize and de-junk your workspace. Set it up so that clutter has less opportunity to accumulate. Devote time regularly to clearing out accumulated junk of all kinds: paperwork, old e-mail messages, and so forth. Make sure your business tools serve you; you should not serve them. If floods of e-mails and voice messages are gobbling up your time, put limits on them.

a note from
the instructor

RESOURCES FOR SPACE CLEARING

One of the best ways to generate positive chi is to get rid of the clutter that's impeding its flow. You'll be amazed at the effect it has on your mood to clear away all the junk that's been weighing you down. If you need help organizing your space-clearing efforts, you'll find the following resources helpful:

- *Clear Your Clutter with Feng Shui*, by Karen Kingston (Derry, NH: Broadway Books, 1999).
- *The Learning Annex Presents Uncluttering Your Space* by the Learning Annex and Ann Sullivan (New York: NY: John Wiley & Sons, 2004).

Pay special attention to your interaction with others. Remember that what you put forth is on its way back to you—including gossip and unnecessary criticism. Respect the individual chi of others. Radiate goodwill to all those with whom you interact.

Clear the air and reactivate the flow of good chi after every negative interaction. Refuse to let the sha chi of others throw away the positive chi you've worked so hard to cultivate. The most powerful influence on your chi at any given time is not what people or circumstances do to it, but the way you respond to them. Choose to respond to bad situations in a positive, upbeat way; be confident that a solution will present itself; and let go of the negative feelings. Never give them a chance to accumulate!

Now that we've seen some of the basics of good career feng shui, let's look at some of the things you can do to cultivate specific attributes in your career.

Assertiveness

Do you have difficulty taking the initiative at work? Do you wish you could "take charge" of a situation more readily, or leap at opportunities as they come by? Feng shui may be able to help.

If you want to become more assertive in your business dealings, boost the yang energy in your office, home, and personal life. Bring in more crisp, bright lighting—especially lighting that focuses upward, to lift yang chi. Add a touch of fire in the Knowledge area, or use some blue to enhance your wisdom and self-awareness. Place your desk in the powerful command position, with your back to a wall, facing your office door—but of course, not in a direct line with the door. To hone your competitive edge and become more assertive, wear crisp whites and surround yourself with metal symbolism.

Recognition

Do you feel as though people and opportunities are passing you by? Does it seem that no matter how hard you work, the kudos always seem to go to somebody else? You may need help in the recognition department.

If you're trying to get noticed, wear bright purple, silk, and stars. To boost your charisma, wear shiny reds. Minister to the Fame area of your home and office with plenty of fire symbolism.

Knowledge

Are you out of the loop at work? Do you feel you're lacking a certain savvy when it comes to your chosen field? Feng shui can help enhance the flow of information and knowledge, and can assist in your ability to apply them.

To enhance wisdom and knowledge, wear dark, rich blues, and enhance the blue accents in your office. Adjust your books and reference materials so that they're highly visible and close at hand. Add a little more metal, to help information reach you clearly.

People Skills

Do you find it difficult to interact with people on the job? Do you have trouble eliciting cooperation from coworkers? Do people have trouble opening up to you? Feng shui can improve your people skills by addressing several areas of the ba-gua.

To enhance your communications with others, boost energy levels in the Relationships, Family, and Helpful People areas of your workspace. To attract more help from coworkers, wear gray or accessorize with jewelry bearing the colors that represent the six syllables of the Buddha's Mantra (Om Ma Ni Pad Me Hum): white, red, yellow, green, blue, and black. Wearing and decorating with yellows and browns will help you develop empathy for others.

Opportunity

Do you feel that promotions, projects, and deals are passing you by? Feng shui has much to say about opportunity, which it views as being nearly synonymous with healthy chi flow and the influx of wealth. Grow bamboo (rich in opportunity symbolism) at home, both inside and outside, but if you plant it outdoors, keep it well away from walls and foundations, because it spreads quickly. Your best bet is to grow bamboo in a pot, even outdoors, so that it remains contained.

Place a pot of tall, upright bamboo in your office as well. Enhance the front doors of both your home and office with a metal wind chime to "call in" more opportunities or a crystal ball to attract them.

FENG SHUI LESSON-END QUESTIONS

Lesson #7:

1. Describe the chi of your workplace.

_____

_____

_____

2. What Feng Shui adjustments could you perform to improve it?

_____

_____

_____

3. What aspects of your career could use improvement?

_____

_____

_____

4. What practical steps could you take to improve these aspects?

_____

_____

_____

5. What Feng Shui adjustments could you make to assist your efforts?

_____

_____

_____

Other Thoughts:

_____

_____

_____

_____

_____

_____

feng shui for wealth

What Is Wealth? • Setting Financial Goals •
How to Attract Wealth Chi

Feng shui places a great deal of emphasis on wealth, both on gaining it and maintaining it. The casual observer might conclude that feng shui practitioners are greedy and obsessed with material possessions, but nothing could be further from the truth.

In feng shui, wealth does not translate to great monetary riches and financial excess. Feng shui wealth is primarily associated with a sense of abundance and an absence of want, which can, in theory, be achieved at almost any financial level. In fact, feng shui acknowledges that there are many types of wealth and many ways of being wealthy, and that not all people need or desire the same type.

Now that we've placed this topic in its proper context, let's look at a few of the ways that feng shui can enhance your wealth.

BEGIN WITH THE PRACTICAL

If you're seeking to increase your income, hang on to more of what you make, and get higher returns on your investments, feng shui can add a profitable new dimension to your efforts.

Here, as in all aspects of your life, feng shui shouldn't be used as a substitute for common sense and practical action. It can't guarantee you wealth, and it's unlikely to help you much if you're not willing to take practical steps to assure your financial well-being. But if you arm yourself with sound financial knowledge, practice fiscal responsibility, and actively work toward realistic goals, having good feng shui can boost your efforts.

If your goal is better monetary health, first take a long, hard look at your financial life. Make a list of practical ways you could generate more income and cut expenses. Go through your investments and get a realistic picture of their performance; then research possible ways to get a better return. These pragmatic steps must come first.

Next, check your attitude. Do you worry constantly about not having enough, even though your income has risen steadily over the past decade? Do you have an aversion to looking at your finances closely? Many of us are constrained financially, not because of the actual state of our finances but because of our *attitudes* toward money.

If we're constantly afraid that we won't be able to meet our financial needs, we'll never believe that we have enough money, not even when we have millions in the bank. Maybe your problem isn't really the amount of money in your bank account but the way you're thinking and feeling about your money. If you're burdening your financial health with negative money attitudes, you must address these first before feng shui can be of much help.

CLARIFY YOUR FINANCIAL GOALS

Next, assess your financial needs and decide just how much *is* enough. There's no rule saying you have to stop acquiring wealth when you reach that goal, only that you've agreed in advance what amount you're aiming for. Remember that the more specifically you define your goals, the more likely you will be to achieve them. Where do you see yourself headed financially? Where would you like to be? Visualize the lifestyle you would like to lead.

If you met your goal, maybe you'd continue to live at about the same standard you do today but would be able to retire from a job that merely produces income to pursue your true passion, to spend more time with your family, or to do charitable work. Maybe you envision having enough extra cash to set up a charitable trust. You could have any number of reasons to accumulate wealth that have nothing to do with greed or self-indulgence.

Next, take a realistic look at where you are today. List the things you need to change in order to get from point A to point B, and commit yourself to doing them. List the personal attributes that attract wealth—assertiveness, integrity, knowledge, ambition, diligence, and social skills—and assess those qualities in yourself. Work on developing any areas in which you consider yourself weak.

When you can honestly state that you're cultivating a healthy financial attitude and taking pragmatic steps toward generating wealth, you can then look to feng shui to enhance your efforts. However, if you're having trouble achieving clarity on your own, you can also start by creating good feng shui in your home and office, which will help you feel better and more balanced. Remember that your space will affect your ability to perform.

 a note from
the instructor

CLEAR YOUR WEALTH AREA
OF STAGNANT CHI

It's extremely important that you become aware of all the factors that may be influencing the chi in your Wealth area. Any negative, draining, or stagnating elements may have detrimental effects on your financial health.

A student of mine complained of stagnant finances. His business appeared to be doing well, but somehow the checks never seemed to come in quickly enough. After he took my class, he discovered that he had several boxes of old files and paperwork stacked in the middle of the Wealth area of his home and office, gathering dust. He threw out those useless documents the following afternoon, and within a week, my student reported that a steady stream of checks had begun to arrive—along with money he'd never expected.

ATTRACT WEALTH CHI

Feng shui draws heavily from the culture that produced it. Chinese folklore is replete with symbols of wealth and prosperity. Use them to draw wealth to you, to stimulate cash flow, and to heighten your attention to financial matters.

Deities and Spiritual Guides

You may enhance your career by invoking blessings from your spiritual guides and divine spirits, according to your religious tradition: God, Allah, Jesus Christ, the Virgin Mary, Buddha, saints, guardian angels. Don't be afraid to ask them for guidance and to bless you with the wisdom to know the higher truths (of course, if you're deeply religious, this would be an integral *first* step, not merely an "enhancement"). Place figures of deities in your living room, dining room, kitchen, foyer, den, or office.

Jade "Money" Plants

Jade plants put us in mind of burgeoning wealth because of their swelling, coin-shaped leaves. Place these money magnets in your home and workspace—particularly in the Wealth area. You can keep these plants in any room.

Bamboo

A powerful symbol of prosperity and growth, tall, vigorous bamboo grows steadily skyward, just as we hope our wealth will. Place a tall bamboo plant in your Wealth area. With the rising popularity of feng shui in America, many garden shops carry potted bamboo, often already decorated with red and gold ribbons or other symbols of financial strength. Bamboo is highly effective when placed in any room in your house.

Bamboo also flourishes outdoors in many parts of the country. To create a highly auspicious view, plant a stand of bamboo where it will be visible from your Wealth area. Be sure to keep its roots well away from the foundations of your home, outbuildings, and walls—it's extremely prolific and can burrow into these structures. It's best to plant bamboo only in pots to keep it under control.

Wind Chimes or Crystal Balls

In the Helpful Friends area of your office or home, hang metal wind chimes or faceted crystal balls enhanced with the colors of the six syllables of the Buddha's mantra, as mentioned in Lesson 7: Om Ma Ni Pad Me Hum (white, red, yellow, green, blue, and black).

These objects attract benefactors who will assist you in getting your next promotion or landing a new, more rewarding job. These supportive people can also be instrumental in helping you find money-making or career opportunities. Hang wind chimes outside on the eaves of your house; at missing corners indoors, you can also add wind chimes, or crystal balls.

Water Flow, Cash Flow

Flowing water subtly suggests flowing money. Place cheerfully bubbling fountains in areas of your home or office devoted to finances. But make sure the water flows toward the heart of your home, not away from it. It's auspicious to live where natural, clean water flows gently past your home.

Coins on a Red Cloth

Red is a symbol of good luck and life. It's full of expansive, fiery energy. Anything touching or surrounded by red is augmented and ignited. A traditional feng shui wealth attractor is a collection of shiny coins arranged on a red cloth. Place the pile of coins in a highly visible part of your Wealth area, where they'll remind you often of the wealth you're seeking. Use any coins that say "prosperity" to you, whether they're specially made Chinese coins purchased from a feng shui shop, reproduction Spanish doubloons, or a pile of sparkling new dimes. Place them in any parts of your house devoted to wealth and finances, especially in the Wealth area of your home's ba-gua.

Ten-Emperors Coins

These are replicas of coins from China's ten emperors, and you can find them at many feng shui shops. The coins should be strung together with a red cord and hung on a yellow, imperial-colored cloth. They're extremely potent when placed in the Wealth corner of your home or office. They can also cure the negative chi caused by asymmetrical shapes in your home's lot; place a string of Ten-Emperors coins in each corner of your property.

Dragons

The dragon is the premier symbol of good fortune in Chinese culture. The mere presence of dragon images and figures is said to attract the luckiest chi. Feng shui masters often wear images of dragons on their clothing to carry the mystical creature's protection with them wherever they go. Dragon images in your home and office draw the kind of powerful chi that stimulates vigorous wealth.

A red, green, or purple dragon is particularly auspicious—traditional Chinese culture associates these colors with wealth. A dragon playing with a pearl is an especially potent wealth attractor.

Dragons often take on the form of terrestrial animals. A tortoise dragon, for example, symbolizes wealth and longevity; a horse dragon attracts wealth and recognition. A phoenix dragon, an extremely favorable creature, calls forth money-making opportunities.

Choose décor that features dragon images: statues, figurines, tapestries, plates, vases, and other ornaments. Place dragon symbolism throughout your home, but make sure there's at least one powerful dragon guarding your Wealth area.

Lucky dragon figurine.

Goldfish

Fish are considered lucky because their movement mimics healthy chi. Goldfish in particular are believed to attract wealth because of their resemblance to their namesake. A body of feng shui commentary addresses the issue of the number of fish you should keep. But there's no such thing as an inauspicious number of fish—provided they're all healthy. In general, though, an odd number of fish attracts more yang energy, the type of chi associated with growth—which is what you want if you're trying to increase your wealth. An even number draws more upon stable yin energy, the type of chi that may help you hang on to the wealth that you have.

The Three-Legged Toad

Many feng shui suppliers sell figurines featuring a three-legged toad with a coin in its mouth, a character from a famous ancient Chinese folktale. According to the story, the toad, upon being rescued from a well, brought its benefactor an endless series of gold coins from a hidden pile of treasure. The toad figurine represents money coming to you from a vast, unknown source. Place this figure near your door.

Other Auspicious Animals

Chinese culture associates numerous animals with wealth. Bats, particularly red ones, are seen as lucky money magnets. It's good luck to have bats roosting in or near your home, but even images of bats can work in your favor.

The crane symbolizes both longevity and fortune. It's featured beautifully in much of Chinese art.

Golden elephants, whether depicted as figurines or in paintings, represent a caravan bringing wealth to your doorstep.

Finally, the tortoise symbolizes wealth, among many other good things. If a tortoise wanders into your house, it's a sign of imminent good fortune. Help this auspicious creature find its way in, symbolically, by placing a tortoise figurine in your home. These figurines make excellent additions to any room.

Semiprecious Stones

Colorful, polished stones, like jade, topaz, amethyst, and rose quartz (among many others), have the appearance of precious jewels. They naturally incline the mind toward wealth. Jade is particularly rich in wealth symbolism. Emperors and wealthy Chinese nobles used it extensively in their palaces.

Many gift shops offer loose, polished, semiprecious stones for a few dollars a scoop. Choose stones that don't have too many rough, jagged edges and pointed shapes. Place your stones in an ornate pot, preferably a deep one that gives the impression of wealth and prosperity. Position these stones in any room of your home.

Your Ship Has Come In

In many traditional Chinese homes, you'll find a small model sailing ship—or a picture of a ship—laden with gold. This ship brings wealth to your household. Load up your wealth-bringing ship with gold coins and imitation gold ingots (available at feng shui supply shops). You can place this ship model anywhere in your home, but it's especially effective where water energy is needed. Just make sure that your ship points toward the center of your home—you don't want your ship sailing off with all your hard-earned wealth!

Wealth Colors

Green, purple, red, and gold inspire wealth. Energize your Wealth area and other parts of your home with these money-friendly colors.

Green is the color of growth, of vigorous, active, growing things—a wise color to use if you would like your finances to grow and remain healthy. Red is an intensifier; it ignites whatever it touches and draws attention to whatever it surrounds. It's also the primary color associated with protection and good luck. Purple is associated with royalty and nobility. The symbolism of the color gold needs no explanation—just make sure it's a true metallic gold, not just dark yellow.

Choose predominantly bright reds, vibrant greens, rich purples, and shining, sparkling golds. Shiny, metallic versions of these colors (as in silk fabric and lacquer paint) are most effective.

Your Personal Treasure

Traditional Chinese people who wish to become wealthy often keep a container of wealth symbols somewhere in their home or office. You can create your own "treasure chest" out of nearly any container and fill it with items that symbolize wealth to you.

Earthenware vessels are best, since the earth produces gold, but crystal and metal also work well. Perhaps best of all is a gourd, itself a symbol of wealth.

The size of your future fortune will not necessarily correspond to the size of the container you use. As always, it's the "size" and clarity of your intentions that make this exercise effective.

Fill the container with symbols of prosperity. Use polished semi-precious stones, like quartz, lapis lazuli, amethyst, citrine, and topaz. Even a handful of uncooked rice works—food nourishes your ability to achieve prosperity. Or, if you use a vase, you can add a bunch of bamboo plants and water to "grow" your wealth.

Bowl with symbols of wealth.

FENG SHUI LESSON-END QUESTIONS

Lesson #8:

1. What is your own personal definition of wealth? Describe not only a dollar amount, but also the type of lifestyle, assets, investments, and so forth that you would need to have in order to feel wealthy.

_____

_____

_____

_____

_____

2. How does your current financial situation differ from what you've written above?

_____

_____

_____

_____

_____

3. List pragmatic steps you could take to improve your finances.

_____

_____

_____

_____

_____

4. List Feng Shui adjustments you could perform to assist your efforts.

_____

_____

_____

_____

_____

Other Thoughts:

_____

_____

_____

_____

_____

_____

feng shui for health

Best Practices for Good Heath • Balancing Yin and Yang Chi
• Feng Shui Cures for Specific Health Problems

FENG SHUI AND YOUR HEALTH

For centuries, people have turned to feng shui to improve and maintain their health. Feng shui addresses the "bigger picture" of health (the total scope of the individual's environment and other influences) rather than the single symptom. With its ties to traditional Chinese medicine, feng shui recognizes the connection between body and environment, and the profound influence the health of one can have on the health of the other. The Black Sect school of feng shui also acknowledged the connection between mind and body before the notion became popular in Western culture.

But while feng shui has occasionally been credited with miraculous cures, its effects are usually subtle. Just as it does with wealth and career, having good feng shui simply enhances your practical efforts.

It requires pragmatic action and sensible motivations to be effective. You can't live on cheeseburgers and root beer, watch 8 hours of television a day, and then expect a few simple feng shui remedies to bring you vibrant health. But if you live a balanced, healthy lifestyle and get regular exercise, nutrition, and medical checkups, you'll find feng shui knowledge an auspicious partner in the care of your health.

Let's look first at some of the ways feng shui views health, and then examine the specific feng shui enhancements and remedies you can use to boost your health and aid in healing.

Yin and Yang Health

Traditional Chinese medicine sees health in terms of yin and yang energies: Healthy people have balanced yin and yang; sick people suffer from too much, or too little, of one or the other.

In centuries past, whole encyclopedias of illnesses were described as symptoms of imbalanced yin or yang. Ancient Chinese medicine divided the body itself into yin and yang regions—the internal organs were predominantly yin; the muscles and skin, predominantly yang.

Much of what feng shui has to say about our health still follows this model. It recommends that we maintain a balance of yin and yang forces in our lives in order to enjoy optimal health.

When we're not getting enough yang, we feel sluggish and depressed. We may suffer from poor circulation, and our joints may eventually develop the problems associated with disuse. When we've got an overdose of yang, we may become jittery, hyperactive, or overly aggressive, leaving ourselves vulnerable to stress-related illnesses.

If our chi carries too much yin, we may feel weak; our immune system may not work properly, and injuries may be slow to heal. Too little yin may cause insomnia.

When yin and yang are balanced, we feel calm and energized, capable, clear-minded, cheerful, and peaceful—in short, the ideal state for good health.

Foster healthy yin with regular rest and sleep patterns. Organize your life so that you have time to relax and wind down from your day. Encourage vibrant yang with proper exercise and mental stimulation.

Create a relaxing environment in yin spaces (bedrooms) with soothing lighting and décor; stimulate vibrant energy in yang spaces (living rooms, recreation rooms) with bright light and cheerful colors.

Healthy Chi Flow

Chi moves through your body along pathways called *meridians*, and enters and exits through gateways called *chakras*, located at the top of your head, midbrain, throat, heart, stomach, navel, and sex organs. The chakra at the top of your head is the most important—it's your closest

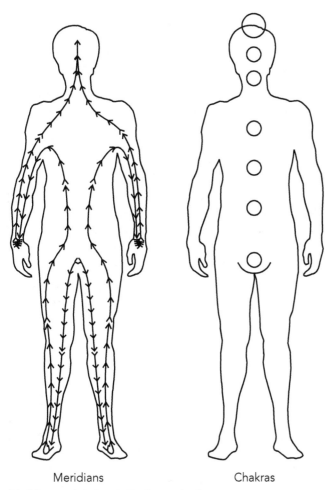

Meridians   Chakras

Meridians and chakras in the human body.

connection to the energy of the heavens. A vigorous flow of beneficial chi through these energy pathways and centers is vital to good health. Acupuncturists explain numerous health problems as manifestations of blocked chi in the body. The cures they perform liberate the chi, allowing the pathway to clear and the illness to heal.

a note from
the instructor

CHRONIC HEALTH PROBLEMS? YOUR HOME MAY BE HARBORING NEGATIVE CHI

A client asked for my help because she had been suffering from chronic fatigue for several years. She suspected that some aspect of her home was the culprit.

Immediately, I saw that the shape of her home was problematic: a "dust-pan" shape, wider at the front than at the back, which rendered it unable to hang on to beneficial chi. But I suspected a more severe problem. This was more than a case of "not enough good stuff." My client was suffering genuine harm from some element in her home.

We scoured the entire house for the offending object, ending our search in her bedroom. Under her bed, I discovered a mound of cardboard boxes jammed tightly into every available inch of space.

"Here's your problem," I told her. "First, chi can't circulate under your bed as you sleep. You're not getting the rejuvenating energy you need."

"I never feel rested when I wake up in the morning," she admitted. "And I seem to have a lot of depressing dreams."

"What do you keep in those boxes?"

"Oh, it's all the 'things' my mother gave me that I didn't want," she told me with a bitter edge to her voice. "For some reason she insisted that I take them."

That was the reason she felt so drained! She was keeping all her worst feelings right under the space where she made herself most vulnerable at night. She wisely moved the boxes, and donated much of the contents to charity, where they helped those in need—a perfect way to turn around bad chi is by creating something positive from it.

Shortly thereafter, she began running daily, and today runs regularly and teaches yoga.

Scour your home for negative chi, particularly if you have any health concerns. Any objects that bring you bad memories or cause you pain are not worth keeping—even if they're worth a lot of money or have sentimental value. Make sure that the only possessions you keep are those that bring you healthful chi and pleasant memories.

Maintain a healthy flow of chi within your body by exercising regularly, eating a balanced diet, drinking plenty of water, getting regular sleep, and avoiding stress.

Quantity of Chi

Vibrant health requires a certain "rate of flow": The chi moving through our bodies must not be too slow or too rapid. Low-level, slow, or stagnant chi causes depression. Exercise and increased activity will stimulate chi flow. On the other extreme, intense, chaotic, and attacking chi causes tension and anxiety. To calm overactive chi, meditate daily, breathe deeply and slowly, and introduce more soothing energy to your thoughts, attitudes, and environments.

Quality of Chi

The most healthful chi flows from growing, living things. Try to spend as much of your time as you can in a natural environment—or one that's arranged to simulate nature—with plenty of fresh air, green plants, moving water, and gentle, stimulating sights and sounds.

Avoid harmful chi; banish it from your environment whenever you find it. Don't dwell on negative thoughts or emotions. Minimize your dealings with chaotic, deceitful, or frustrating people. Long-term exposure to negative chi can have grave consequences on your health.

BEST BETS FOR GOOD HEALTH

Start with the obvious. Be sure you're giving yourself optimal nutrition and exercise, and that your attitudes and lifestyle are conducive to good health. Then consider the following.

Healthy Environments

Bright, sunny, well-ventilated homes and workspaces are best. It's imperative that your environment be clean, dry, in good repair, well organized, and clutter free. Plants, happy pets, and soothing, energizing music attract the kinds of chi that promotes good health. Give yourself and your environment frequent infusions of positive, loving chi from family and friends.

Avoid EMFs

Electromagnetic fields, which are created by anything electric, have long been a suspected culprit in poor health. Don't put electric things too close to where people sit or sleep. Avoid putting computers and television sets in bedrooms. Don't allow electric cables to run under beds. Place plants next to your computer to absorb and counter some of its harmful chi.

Enhance Your Ba-Gua Health Area

Given that good health is central to life, the Health area is central to the home. As you may remember from Lesson 2, the ba-gua octagon is composed of nine areas: eight areas corresponding to its sides, and the Health area (tai chi) in the middle. When the ba-gua is superimposed on the layout of your home, this places the Health area in your home's center point.

Bring earthy materials and symbols, along with bright light, into the middle of your home: pottery, clay, and earthy colors. Avoid clutter in this area and keep it meticulously clean.

Decorate with Health and Longevity Symbols

In traditional Chinese culture, health was nearly synonymous with longevity. To this day, Chinese artwork is replete with symbols of a long and healthy life. These symbols around your home may enhance your own health and longevity chi.

Tortoises and cranes are considered extremely long-lived, gifted with the fortunate chi of longevity. Pine and bamboo, because they're green year-round, symbolize long life. Peaches and mushrooms, once believed to bestow immortality, also feature prominently in Chinese artwork. Scenes depicting spring, with its connotations of rebirth and renewal, are also auspicious reminders of good health.

student experience

"I found I was always feeling under the gun at work, often working 10-hour days without time to leave for lunch. I've tried to make small changes. I put a bamboo plant in my office and allow myself five-minute breaks to close my eyes, breath deeply, and relax. I really feel that even these small steps are making a big difference in my stress levels."

—Steve, tax consultant

Pine Trees

Bamboo

Peaches

Mushrooms

Cranes

Tortoises

Longevity images in Chinese culture.

FENG SHUI CURES FOR HEALTH CONCERNS

Feng shui does not generally offer specific cures for medical problems; instead, it helps you create a beneficial, peaceful environment in which you're more likely to remain healthy. For instance, it offers the Great Sunshine Buddha Meditation (for more details, see Lesson 12), which is an excellent way to enhance your personal chi and, by logical extension, your health. It also helps you avoid situations that may threaten your health, like exposure to EMFs.

But although there are no explicit cures for individual diseases, certain aspects of feng shui do concern particular regions of the body. Each major organ of the body relates to a specific element. When you develop problems in an organ, you may be lacking adequate nourishment from its corresponding element, or you may be living with too much of the element that controls it.

Let's take a look at several major organs and their corresponding elements, and examine the feng shui remedies you can perform to strengthen that organ's health.

Heart

The heart's element is fire. Every symbol (color, shape, season, and so forth) related to fire is also associated with the heart. If you lack fire energy in your home, boost your heart's health by adding more fiery symbols to your environment: candles, triangles, and summertime images. Decorate with red tones, and add a few orange and yellow accents. If there's too much fire, tone it down with some water energy.

Certain foods carry the symbolic energy of fire. To boost heart health, enjoy "reddish" foods such as tomatoes, strawberries, red peppers, red cabbage, shrimp, and lobster.

Lungs

The lungs are closely associated with metal, perhaps because of metal's association with "transactions"—the lungs are constantly exchanging oxygen for carbon dioxide. Help your lungs do their job by enhancing metal symbolism in your life; bring more whites and metallic colors into your environment. Accent your décor with metal objects. A metal chiming clock with a pleasant ticking sound and chime may prove especially beneficial, both because of its material and because the rhythmic ticking mimics the steady rhythm of breathing and moving chi.

You may also want to enrich your diet with foods that carry metal symbolism: potatoes, chicken, fish, scallops, and egg whites.

The Liver

The liver, because of its vital cleansing function, is strongly associated with springtime and renewal and, as a result, is the domain of wood—springtime's element. Promote better liver health with green, growing plant and wood energy. Decorate with vibrant greens and blues. Introduce tall, upward-stretching shapes into your décor: vertical stripes, tall statues and figures, tall furniture and wall hangings.

Feed your liver a diet rich in the foods that carry vibrant green wood energy: spinach, broccoli, celery, and peas.

The Stomach

Because of its central role in our health—and perhaps because of its central location in our bodies—the stomach is associated with earth, the same element that dominates the tai chi center of our homes.

Soothe digestive difficulties with earth symbolism: yellows, golds, russets, and other earthy colors. Decorate with square or rectangular shapes. Enrich your diet with "earthy" foods, like yellow squash, carrots, and eggs.

I'd like to leave you with one final thought on the subject of feng shui and your health: None of what we've discussed here should substitute for the advice of a competent physician. If you suspect that you have a health problem, by all means see a doctor. Get appropriate medical care first, and follow your doctor's advice—*even if it conflicts with what you've read here.* Symbolic remedies are an enhancement, a helpmate to your regular health regimen. They must never be a substitute for professional medical care.

For more information on feng shui and your health, check out *Healing with Whole Foods: Oriental Traditions and Modern Nutrition,* by Paul Pitchford (Berkeley, CA: North Atlantic Books, 2002) and *Feng Shui and Health,* by Nancy SantoPietro (New York: Three Rivers Press, 2002).

FENG SHUI LESSON-END QUESTIONS

Lesson #9:

1. How would you describe your overall health?

_____

_____

_____

_____

_____

2. List any "trouble spots" in your lifestyle that could contribute to poor health; for instance, irregular sleep habits, poor diet, lack of exercise, or high stress.

_____

_____

_____

_____

_____

3. List practical changes you could make to your lifestyle to improve these "trouble spots."

_____

_____

_____

_____

_____

4. List Feng Shui adjustments you could make to your lifestyle, routine, and environment that would assist your efforts.

_____

_____

_____

_____

_____

Other Thoughts:

_____

_____

_____

_____

_____

_____

feng shui in relationships

Feng Shui and Romance • Feng Shui and Marriage •
Feng Shui and Family • Feng Shui and Friendship

Feng shui recognizes the importance of our connection to one another. Our relationships bring us joy, comfort, and opportunities, and help us define and discover who we are. Relationships are so vital to our fortunes that five of the eight ba-gua areas are directly devoted to our connections to others: Family, Fame, Marriage, Children, and Helpful People. Let's take a closer look at the ways feng shui can help us strengthen our relationships.

FENG SHUI AND FRIENDSHIP

Feng shui takes a broad view of friendship. The category of Helpful People, the bottom-right area of the ba-gua (see Lesson 2), includes everyone from bosses and mentors to neighbors and business associates. Helpful People are some of the primary conduits of good fortune and opportunity, and among the best buffers for misfortune. It's extremely difficult to get through life without a network of friends, and even the most fortunate among us could benefit from greater friendship.

The ba-gua devotes an entire area to the cultivation of friends and allies, yet most people's homes and businesses don't make much use of the potential symbolic power of this area. Enhance your Helpful People area with a metal wind chime, crystal ball, or some form of the six syllables of the Buddha's mantra: Om Ma Ni Pad Me Hum (we discuss this mantra in greater detail in Lesson 12). Or hang photos of your family, friends, and benefactors.

Orient yourself to draw friendly chi by adjusting your attitude; resolve to become more open to friendships, and take positive ongoing action to nurture the ones you have. Be generous in sharing your good fortune with your friends and colleagues. The old adage of "What goes around comes around" couldn't be more accurate. Be a source of uplifting chi for your friends and acquaintances; radiate positive energy toward them and surround them with good thoughts. It's the nature of an intimately connected universe that what you send forth eventually radiates back to you.

FENG SHUI AND ROMANCE

Although feng shui probably won't bring you the lover of your dreams, it *can* smooth the path to romance. It can help you attract a new lover or heighten the romance of the relationship you're in.

Because of its intimate ties to family-oriented Chinese culture, feng shui sees romance as a prelude to marriage and family. It attracts romance by accumulating good family chi. You don't need to have marriage and family as your immediate goal to use feng shui to boost your love life, but you may have to adapt some of the ways you use its symbolism if you're not aiming for marriage and a family.

Start with internal work: Clarify what kind of relationship you want and work to clear any mental, emotional, or behavioral barriers. Putting yourself in the right mental space to begin a new relationship can be challenging, but feng shui can help you along the way. See Lesson 14 for ways to align your personal chi with your goals.

Use feng shui to guide you as you prepare your external space to welcome your new relationship. Adjust your inner and outer chi to the new reality of your life *before* that reality enters so that when the opportunity arrives, it will find a home.

a note from
the instructor

A CLIENT'S SEARCH FOR ROMANCE

Be careful with the symbolism you place in your home. Whether you recognize its effect or not, your environment may influence the type of relationship you're drawn to.

A frustrated client once called me for relationship advice: "Either all the guys I date are not too bright, or they're intellectually stimulating but physically unattractive! Is it too much to hope that I could find a guy who turns me on physically but still has something interesting to say?"

You wouldn't believe what I found in her living room. The first thing that caught my eye was this enormous armoire—right in the center of her relationship area. I'd never seen such a thing. It took up half a wall and stretched all the way to the ceiling. There was no room for anything—or any*one*—else. That had to be at least part of her problem.

But then my eyes were drawn to the objects she had placed near the massive armoire. I almost laughed out loud. The armoire stood next to two Romanesque statues: one, a body without a head; the other, a head with no body! And that was exactly the kind of men she was attracting!

I advised her to get rid of the statues immediately. She moved them to a closet that day, and disposed of them the following week. A few months later she met a handsome, intelligent man, the love of her life.

Making a Living Space Right for Two

Many people make the mistake of keeping their home set up for single living, even though they don't wish to remain single. If you truly want to have a relationship with someone, you'll need to make room for two.

Clear out any objects, furnishings, or décor that may harbor the chi of a past relationship. If you must keep a few mementos, pack them away in storage. But don't allow your environment to announce (to yourself or to your new mate) that you haven't truly moved on from your previous relationship.

Make room in a closet for a new partner's clothing, and clear a shelf in the medicine cabinet for his or her toiletries. Adjust your space so that you can be flexible enough to accommodate another person's needs, habits, and presence.

Create areas in your home for the two of you to do things together: Arrange your kitchen so that two can cook, set the dining table up for an intimate dinner for two, and prepare an area just for talking quietly.

a note from
the instructor

IF YOUR HOUSE SAYS "DON'T TOUCH," YOU MAY BE SENDING THE SAME MESSAGE TO PROSPECTIVE PARTNERS

People often seek out feng shui consultants for matters of the heart. A woman once called me because she hadn't had a relationship in many years. When I visited her home, I found it beautifully furnished. As I entered her bedroom, I commented on her gorgeous décor.

"Oh, please don't touch anything," she responded quickly. "I like everything in my bedroom to stay nice."

Therein lay her problem. Her home, like her life, radiated an aura of being untouchable. Prospective mates sensed her unwillingness to be "touched," or to accommodate their presence. Until she was ready to permit the touch of another, she would have to enjoy her beautiful surroundings alone.

Decorate your bedroom to invite romance chi. Place romantic images on the walls, and keep décor items in pairs.

Finally, begin living as if your new mate were already there. Do things as you would if you were accommodating another person. By doing this you're adapting your personal chi to the reality you desire: life with a partner.

FENG SHUI AND MARRIAGE

In feng shui terms, marriage is the ultimate expression of yin and yang in harmony. When a marriage is strong, the yin and yang of both partners are in balance. Since nobody can be entirely yin or entirely yang all the time, this means that the married partners must be responsive enough to each other that when one goes into a yin phase, the other responds by becoming more yang, and vice versa. She must become strong when he's weak; when he leads, she must follow. If both are constantly trying to lead, or both remain passive, the yin and yang will become unbalanced and the relationship slides toward failure. All aspects of the relationship must be balanced; wild passion must alternate with moments of quiet affection.

A feng shui perspective on a troubled marriage identifies the imbalanced element or elements, and attempts to remedy the imbalance by toning down or augmenting the energies that seem to be causing the problem. But the prudent feng shui master wouldn't wait until a problem develops before offering certain courses of action designed to keep a good marriage harmonious.

Here are some specific tips:

- Decorate your Marriage ba-gua area with photos of happy occasions—your honeymoon, wedding, anniversary parties.

- Avoid placing too many pictures of friends and family members in your Marriage area (or in your bedroom, if it's in a different part of the ba-gua).

- You want the focus to remain on the two of you.

- Avoid having a television set or computer in the bedroom because these items detract from the intimacy of loving relationships.

- Keep vibrant and colorful fresh flowers in red, pink, and yellow in your bedroom. Fragrant flowers can invite new relationships or strengthen existing ones.

Can't Stop Arguing?

Do you and your mate bicker constantly? Check your home for doors that bang together. Feng shui tradition states that clashing doors foster discord.

If you can't rehang the doors so that they won't bang, tie a 9-, 18-, or 27-inch red ribbon (multiples of 9 are powerful because 9 is the highest single-digit yang number—odd numbers are yang; even numbers are yin) around each knob. Then cut the ribbon in the middle and let the strings hang loose. As you're cutting and tying the ribbon, visualize that there is no more disharmony in the family and that everyone gets along.

student experience

"Learning the principles of feng shui really helped strengthen my relationship with my husband. So much of it simply involves following the golden rule and treating the other person with respect and dignity. It also really helped us communicate better when we removed the television from our bedroom so that we could talk quietly at the end of the day, rather than mutely fall asleep in front of some late-night programming neither of us really cared about anyway."

—Mary Jane, professional musician

Another solution is to place artwork, figurines, or talismans representing the 12 Chinese zodiac animals (readily available from feng shui supply companies) in the most prominent area of your home or office. Imagine that you're getting along with everyone else and that peace and harmony reigns in the family or office.

Guarding against Infidelity

Obviously, no amount of "furniture arranging" is going to cause a faithful spouse to be disloyal, or an unfaithful one to curb their infidelity. But feng shui *can* influence *tendencies*. Certain configurations inside the home can encourage a discontented spouse's attentions to wander—or can point his or her energies back in the right direction.

Can you see a shed or outbuilding from your bedroom window? Move it. A separate structure outside your Marriage area suggests that one spouse's energies might be going to another "home."

Similarly, don't choose a bedroom with a door leading outside. The symbolic and literal center of your marriage should be safe and protected, deep within your home, and should not appear "easy to leave."

Trying to Conceive?

Check to make sure that the ba-gua area of your home devoted to children (the center right) is not missing or underdeveloped. Enhance the chi of your Children area by adding whites and metals.

 a note from
the instructor

INVITE LUCKY MARRIAGE CHI INTO YOUR LIFE

Marriage chi is considered extremely lucky: It's associated with happiness, harmony, good health, and long life. To attract good marriage chi, wrap nine objects that belong to you in a red cloth and ask a newly married couple to touch or bless them. Be sure to bring objects that are of a non-consumable nature; in other words, don't bring lipstick. Afterward, place the objects in the Marriage corner of your bedroom and leave them there for nine days before using them. It's most effective if you can do this ritual with nine newlywed couples. If you can't find nine *new* couples, identify nine currently married couples who you consider to have loving and lasting relationships. Ask them to bless your nine objects and follow these steps.

Don't store things under your bed, or sweep under it while you're trying to conceive. Feng shui tradition has it that the chi energies that will soon form your new child's life force gather there prior to conception.

It is *not* a good idea to tackle any construction or home remodeling projects during this period. These activities severely disturb a home's chi. Hold off until your new family member has arrived!

FENG SHUI WITH KIDS

Traditionally, there's no such thing as "kids' feng shui." Feng shui recommends the same exercises for children and adults alike. But it makes sense from a feng shui perspective to consider each family member's individual needs, and in that light, children's needs differ from those of adults. Here are some things to watch out for in your children's environment:

Do:

- Create a soothing and comfortable environment for them, to assure restful sleep.

- Place plenty of books and educational items in their environment, but keep them covered if possible.

- Showcase their artwork and achievements.

- Help them develop good feng shui habits: cleanliness, order, and a love of beauty.

Don't:

- Decorate their bedrooms and play rooms with too many bright yang colors, textures, and images—kids need to balance their yin and yang too.

- Place a television set, computer, or video games in their bedroom.

- Decorate their bedroom with violent or "inappropriate" wall posters or paintings.

- Step over their schoolbooks—this disrupts their learning chi.

Clutter is probably the single biggest problem area for children, from a feng shui perspective. Even for adults, clutter can cause energy to stagnate and opportunities to slip away. But for kids, clutter is an even greater hazard because it suppresses their energy and disrupts their growth.

Combat kids' clutter by refusing to let it get a toehold. Don't overburden them with more possessions than they can adequately appreciate and care for. Get into the habit of clearing out unwanted clothes and toys on a regular basis. But do involve them in the decision making: Respect their right to ownership. Make sure they have easy, adequate storage for the possessions they choose to keep.

FENG SHUI AND FAMILY

Feng shui is most effective in bringing family luck and happiness, because the culture that spawned feng shui is itself extremely family oriented. In traditional Chinese culture, a happy family life is central to an individual's well-being. Feng shui seeks to nurture family harmony and closeness, to augment the family fortune, to enhance the luck and fortune of future children, and to safeguard the well-being of each member.

The most important areas of the home to enhance when you're cultivating good family chi are the Family, Love/Relationships, and Children sectors of the ba-gua. Live plants or the colors green and blue are most auspicious for "growing" and enhancing family relations. Place family photos of ancestors and children to bridge different generations and bring them closer. In fact, feng shui recommends displaying happy photos of your family in each of your home's gathering spaces. This is especially important in the living room and dining room, where your family regularly interacts with non-family members. It's important to greet the world with a united front and honor each member of the family.

In addition, you can try this auspicious family luck intensifier: Hang a crystal chandelier in the center of your home, particularly if this is in a family gathering area such as a living room or dining room. Light draws and lifts beneficial yang chi, and the multifaceted crystals magnify and intensify the effect. With this auspicious object hanging in the center (tai chi) of your home—the symbolic heart of your family—you and your loved ones will enjoy excellent family luck.

Improve your use of feng shui by considering each family member's requirements for space, convenience, privacy, and self-expression. Make sure that your home adequately serves each member's needs. Does the avid reader have a quiet, well-lit, book-filled retreat? Can the younger members of the family reach things they need, or do high shelves continually frustrate them? Make certain that family gathering areas include activities and spaces that appeal to each family member.

Here are some tips for curing family strife:

- Calm children's overactive energy with soft materials and soothing colors, like pastel blue and green, and such elements as wood and water.

- Enhance your communication areas in whites, pastels, silver, gold, and metals. Objects made of metal, such as metal sculpture and picture frames, as well as pastel-colored walls, accents, and accessories, are all favorable.

- In areas where conflicts arise, tone down the yang reds, oranges, and hot pinks, and remove any fire symbols (flames, triangles).

FENG SHUI LESSON-END QUESTIONS

Lesson #10:

1. Are you happy with the number and quality of the friendships you have?

_____

_____

_____

2. What pragmatic steps could you take to develop existing friendships and begin new ones?

_____

_____

_____

3. What Feng Shui adjustments could you make to assist your efforts?

_____

_____

_____

4. If you're looking for a mate, describe what you're looking for in a partner and in a relationship. If you're already in a relationship, describe the ways you wish your relationship could be better.

_____

_____

_____

5. What pragmatic steps could you take to invite a new relationship, or to improve the relationship you have?

_____

_____

_____

6. What Feng Shui adjustments could you make to assist your efforts?

_____

_____

_____

7. Describe the ways in which your family life could be more satisfying.

_____

_____

_____

8. What pragmatic steps could you take to make the improvements you listed above?

_____

_____

_____

9. What Feng Shui adjustments could you make to assist your efforts?

_____

_____

_____

Other Thoughts:

_____

_____

_____

_____

_____

_____

your personality and destiny

What Feng Shui Reveals about Your Personality • The Chinese Zodiac • Nine-Star Ki Astrology • How to Harmonize Imbalanced Aspects of Your Personality • How Feng Shui Complements and Enhances Destiny • Choosing Careers and Relationships Compatible with Your Destiny

Feng shui draws its understanding of human personality from its diverse roots in Chinese culture, which is replete with numerous forms of astrology and divination. While Chinese astrology and divination are not integral parts of feng shui, they draw upon many of the same concepts.

We've seen that three sources of energy affect human fortune: tien chai (heaven luck), ren chai (human luck), and ti chai (earth luck). All three forms of luck play a vital role in the expression of an individual's personality.

Tien chai gives us our basic personality structure by "stamping" us with the prevailing energies present at the moment of our birth. It's the most important of the three because our tien chai is all we have to work with—it's the "clay" we must mold to adapt and enhance our personalities to suit the demands life places on us. When we recognize a deficit in our "birth" personalities (our tien chai), we work with our ren chai to improve it. If we're familiar with practical feng shui, we can also work with ti chai to enhance our efforts.

Chinese astrology also recognizes the relative strengths or weaknesses of the five elements at each moment in time. These elements have a profound effect on the innate personality you are born with. For example, people born at a time when fire is particularly potent tend to be emotionally expressive; those born in a strongly earthlike period are apt to become excellent nurturers and caretakers.

Each person possesses at least some trace of each element in his or her personality. The dominant element of an individual's birth year usually determines the primary characteristics of his or her personality, but the elements of one's birth month, day, and hour are also strong contributors.

The way each combination of elements manifests in an individual is a function of the strength or weakness of that element. People who are strongly wood, for example, may become too rigid and inflexible, like the "woody" stems of plants. With too little wood, a person seems to be "ungrounded," blown about by every passing breeze. When wood is balanced, an individual can stick firmly to his or her principles, while still giving appropriate consideration to other points of view. Fortunately, we can adapt our ren chai (and assist our efforts by adapting our ti chai through feng shui) to balance any areas that are too strong or too weak.

Naturally, the unique combinations of these elements in our personalities predispose us to certain types of careers, lifestyles, and interests. They also mean that we're more likely to get along with people whose personality elements are compatible with ours; weak wood people generally find it easy to get along with water people because water supports wood. On the other hand, just as certain elements control or harm other elements, people with certain dominant personalities conflict with certain others. Wood people may feel very uncomfortable in the presence of "cutting" metal personalities.

Chinese astrology is a rich and complex subject, with many facets and schools of thought. We'll touch on a few of these schools throughout this lesson, but for starters, let's take a closer look at the astrological school of thought that's the most similar to Western systems: the Chinese 12-animal zodiac.

THE CHINESE 12-ANIMAL ZODIAC

The Chinese zodiac recognizes a continuous cycle of 12 years, 12 months, and 24 hours. It associates each of these 12 time increments with an animal from Chinese folklore. Each animal possesses a distinct personality, with virtues and "problem areas," and may either naturally get along or naturally clash with any of the other 12 animals. Individuals usually manifest most strongly the traits of their birth-year animal and secondarily the traits of their month and hour animals.

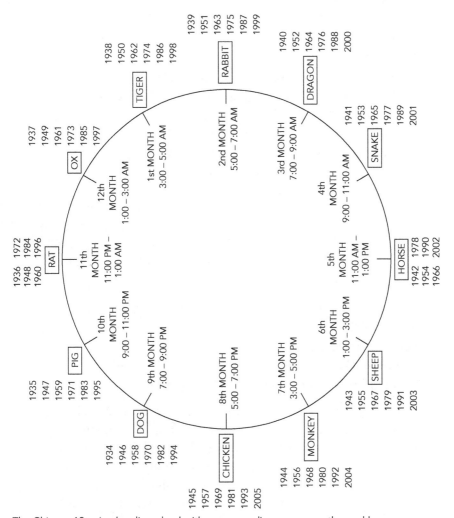

The Chinese 12-animal zodiac wheel with corresponding years, months, and hours.

The zodiac animals' years correspond closely to the years of the Western calendar. For each animal, we've listed the most recent years that occurred in the twentieth century, and several of the years that will occur during the first portion of this century. The cycle repeats every 12 years.

The hours assigned to each animal correspond to a 24-hour cycle. Each animal gets 2 hours per day.

The months are trickier to match with the Western calendar. Some schools of thought link them with a solar calendar, others with a lunar, and still others with various natural signs, such as first frosts and harvest times. In a moment, we list the principal month for each animal, but we'd like you to keep in mind that these animals are not directly linked to a given month.

Each animal is also associated with an element. Remember that the element associated with each animal is simply another layer of meaning—an additional interpretation—not a direct correlation. In other words, a monkey is not associated with water because a monkey is "like water" but because they happen to fall together in the cosmological organization of the zodiac. We discuss the personality aspects of the elements in greater detail later in this lesson.

Rat *(Years: 1900, 1912, 1924, 1936, 1948, 1960, 1972, 1984, 1996, 2008, 2020):* Rats are charming, meticulous, and often shrewd and wise. They can sometimes become greedy, which may lead to their downfall.

Ox *(Years: 1901, 1913, 1925, 1937, 1949, 1961, 1973, 1985, 1997, 2009, 2021):* Like their animal comrade under the yoke, oxen are hardworking and steady. They can be extremely stubborn. Oxen born during the winter will be well cared for in life; those born in summer will toil hard for little return.

Tiger *(Years: 1902, 1914, 1926, 1938, 1950, 1962, 1974, 1986, 1998, 2010, 2022):* Tigers are vibrant, confident, and courageous. They easily become restless and may act rashly— qualities traditional Chinese find highly undesirable in women. Some families avoid having children during tiger years, for fear of bearing a daughter who will grow into a "tiger lady."

Rabbit *(Years: 1903, 1915, 1927, 1939, 1951, 1963, 1975, 1987, 1999, 2011, 2023):* A lucky animal, the rabbit is sensitive, clever, swift, and sociable, but tends to be fickle and aloof.

Dragon *(Years: 1904, 1916, 1928, 1940, 1952, 1964, 1976, 1988, 2000, 2012, 2024):* The luckiest zodiac animals, dragons possess a magical charisma. They tend to experience huge emotional swings, and their mystic loftiness often makes them hard to approach.

Snake *(Years: 1905, 1917, 1929, 1941, 1953, 1965, 1977, 1989, 2001, 2013, 2025):* Also a lucky year, since the snake's nickname is the "little dragon." Snakes are wise, calm, intelligent, and beautiful, but they tend toward laziness and selfishness. They make for dangerous enemies.

Horse *(Years: 1906, 1918, 1930, 1942, 1954, 1966, 1978, 1990, 2002, 2014, 2026):* Ambitious, charming, friendly, and hardworking, but horses may also be tactless, selfish, and impatient.

Ram *(Years: 1907, 1919, 1931, 1943, 1955, 1967, 1979, 1991, 2003, 2015, 2027):* The highly likeable ram is artistic, intelligent, cheerful, and generous. A bit irresponsible, rams often do well in business but poorly in family life. The ram is also known as the sheep or the goat.

Monkey *(Years: 1908, 1920, 1932, 1944, 1956, 1968, 1980, 1992, 2004, 2016, 2028):* Vivacious and funny, monkeys are also extremely intelligent and quick. They're the best problem-solvers. But monkeys can be devious and untrustworthy.

Rooster *(Years: 1909, 1921, 1933, 1945, 1957, 1969, 1981, 1993, 2005, 2017, 2029.):* Like their namesake, roosters are brash, sociable, and full of confidence. They may add a flair to social events, but they may also overdo it, becoming garrulous and arrogant.

Dog *(Years: 1910, 1922, 1934, 1946, 1958, 1970, 1982, 1994, 2006, 2018, 2030):* Faithful, vigilant, affectionate, and steadfast, dogs make the best friends. They can suffer from anxiety, because they're constantly on guard.

Pig *(Years: 1911, 1923, 1935, 1947, 1959, 1971, 1983, 1995, 2007, 2019, 2031):* Generally a lucky animal, pigs are both sensitive and self-indulgent. Although they possess a certain social refinement, they can be weak and helpless.

a note from
the instructor

THE 12 CHINESE ZODIAC ANIMALS:
GOOD AND BAD MATCHES

Animal	Good Matches	Bad Matches
Rat	Ox, dragon, monkey	Ram, horse, rooster
Ox	Rat, snake, rooster	Horse, ram, dog
Tiger	Pig, dog, horse	Snake, monkey
Rabbit	Dog, ram, pig	Dragon, horse, rooster
Dragon	Rooster, rat, monkey	Rabbit, dog, ram
Snake	Ox, rooster, monkey	Tiger, pig
Horse	Dog, tiger, ram	Ox, rat
Ram	Horse, rabbit, pig	Rat, ox, dog
Monkey	Snake, rat, dragon	Pig, tiger, snake
Rooster	Dragon, ox, snake	Dog, rabbit, rat
Dog	Rabbit, horse, tiger	Rooster, dragon, ox
Pig	Ram, rabbit, tiger	Monkey, snake

NINE-STAR KI ASTROLOGY
AND YOUR BIRTH YEAR

Nine-star ki astrology is not itself feng shui, but it is closely related. It's a Japanese form of astrology that makes use of similar concepts. Also known as nine-house, nine-star ki astrology is based on the ancient belief that the energy of the universe is filtered through nine important stars, each of which imparts its own unique characteristics on the chi flowing past. These nine stars range from yin to yang, with Vega the farthest on the yin end of the spectrum, and Polaris, the most yang.

Like the animal zodiac, each of the nine stars rules a year and a month. Each star also has a day. Each star belongs to a particular element, with all of that element's qualities and associations. If you've read the previous lessons in this book, you're already familiar with the basic characteristics of fire, earth, metal, water, and wood. Understanding the way the five elements manifest in personality is simply a matter of adapting those same qualities to the human psyche.

Every person is born under a particular year star, month star, and day star. The combination of the unique "chi signatures" of these three stars determines the structure of one's personality. An individual's full nine ki numbers appear in a three-number string: year, month, and day. Your year star determines your fundamental nature. Your month star indicates your character—who you are when the chips are down. Your day star represents the impression you make on others.

For the scope of this book, we focus on your year star, since it's the most influential of your three stars. The full calculation and interpretation of your nine ki numbers, and what they portend for you in the future, is a complex undertaking. If you're interested in having a full nine ki reading, consult a qualified astrologer. See Appendix A for more information.

Finding Your Nine-Star Ki Birth Star

Find the number and element that correspond to your birth year. Keep in mind that in nine-star ki, a year goes not from January 1 to December 31, but from February 4 to February 3 (so if you were born in January, your year star belongs to the previous calendar year):

9 Fire: 1901, 1910, 1919, 1928, 1937, 1946, 1955, 1964, 1973, 1982, 1991, 2000, 2009, 2018

8 Earth: 1902, 1911, 1920, 1929, 1938, 1947, 1956, 1965, 1974, 1983, 1992, 2001, 2010, 2019

7 Metal: 1903, 1912, 1921, 1930, 1939, 1948, 1957, 1966, 1975, 1984, 1993, 2002, 2011, 2020

6 Metal: 1904, 1913, 1922, 1931, 1940, 1949, 1958, 1967, 1976, 1985, 1994, 2003, 2012, 2021

5 Earth: 1905, 1914, 1923, 1932, 1941, 1950, 1959, 1968, 1977, 1986, 1995, 2004, 2013, 2022

4 Wood: 1906, 1915, 1924, 1933, 1942, 1951, 1960, 1969, 1978, 1987, 1996, 2005, 2014, 2023

3 Wood: 1907, 1916, 1925, 1934, 1943, 1952, 1961, 1970, 1979, 1988, 1997, 2006, 2015, 2024

2 Earth: 1908, 1917, 1926, 1935, 1944, 1953, 1962, 1971, 1980, 1989, 1998, 2007, 2016, 2025

1 Water: 1909, 1918, 1927, 1936, 1945, 1954, 1963, 1972, 1981, 1990, 1999, 2008, 2017, 2026

Now that you've identified your birth star, let's look at the characteristics of each star in broad strokes. In the next section, we explore the personalities associated with each element in greater detail. For further reading, refer to *Feng Shui Astrology*, by Takashi Yoshikawa (York Beach, ME: Samuel Weiser Inc., 1986).

1 White Water: The yang manifestation of this star is independent, capable, and highly social. The yin aspect is intelligent and intuitive.

2 Black Earth: This highly yin star produces excellent nurturers; steadfast and selfless.

3 Jade Wood: Highly yang, volatile, energetic, on the cutting edge of change.

4 Green Wood: Mostly yin, self-assured, practical, flexible.

5 Yellow Earth: A balance of yin and yang, powerful and persistent.

6 White Metal: More yin than yang, charismatic, stylish, refined.

7 Red Metal: Very yang, charismatic, affable, a great conversationalist.

8 White Earth: Mostly yin, adventurous, persistent, parsimonious.

9 Purple Fire: The yang aspect of this star is extremely outgoing and ostentatious; the yin aspect is introverted and keenly imaginative.

Note that each star number is associated with both an element and a color, and that it's either predominantly yin or yang, or has facets of both. Star 5, Yellow Earth, stands as the exception to this rule, balancing equal parts yin and yang.

Now let's take a closer look at the ways these elements may manifest in your personality.

The Five Elements and Your Personality

Throughout this book we've dipped into the five elements to enhance or adjust the mood, energy, and focus of an area in your home or workspace; we've even seen how the elements and their related symbols may affect your health. Now that you've identified your own personality structure with a given element, we focus on what that element reveals about who you are:

Fire: Fire people are naturally emotional and expressive. They show a special felicity with etiquette and fashion. Those who express a particularly yang brand of fire can become aggressive; those with yin fire are often introverted, secretly burning like a forge within.

Earth: Earth people are natural caretakers; they typically make nurturing parents and caring medical professionals. They're trustworthy, pragmatic, and "down to earth."

Metal: Metal people are righteous, dependable, precise, and often extremely effective communicators. They're capable of admirable willpower. Their powers of reasoning coupled with their ability to communicate make them powerful leaders.

Water: The water element manifests in two aspects: "still" and "moving." Those who are more inclined to the still aspect tend to be "deep," reflective, contemplative, and wise. Moving water people are highly motivated and sociable, but sometimes a bit unstable.

Wood: Wood people are kind and strongly principled. They can be rigid and inflexible. When their element is well balanced, they are both deeply "rooted" and capable of bending to adapt to new situations.

If you don't identify strongly with the elemental personality of your birth year star, it may be that your month or day star dominates. Most often, our year star places the most noticeable stamp on us, but it's by no means the only influence. If you're curious to learn more, contact a feng shui consultant for a detailed nine-star ki reading.

a note from
the instructor

ELEMENTAL BODY SHAPES

Chinese philosophers first noticed it centuries ago: The stars, and their associated elements, leave their stamp on more than our personalities. The shapes of our bodies often tend to resemble the shapes associated with our birth star elements:

Fire: Broad hips, tapered torso, narrow shoulders and head
Earth: Broad, square, wide-shouldered
Metal: Solid, wiry, pale-skinned
Water: Plump, round, and "flowing"
Wood: Tall, thin

HOW PERSONALITY ELEMENTS INTERACT

As each of the five elements either "nourishes" or "controls" another, individuals belonging to each element interact with people of other elements in predictable ways. Earth people get along well with fire people, as a general rule, because fire nourishes earth. Similarly, wood people find most water people comfortable to be around, but fire people may "burn them up," and metal people can "rub them the wrong way."

But this isn't always the case. People who strongly identify with a given element may sometimes find that the controlling element helps temper the more extreme aspects of their nature. Rushing water people may find the influence of an earth person calming. Strong wood personalities might benefit from the judicious "pruning" they receive from a metal person. They say opposites do attract—sometimes the best remedy for a strong element in our personality may be someone whose personality balances ours.

HARMONIZING IMBALANCED ASPECTS OF YOUR PERSONALITY

Most of us have a clearly dominant element in our personalities, but the most balanced individuals among us have a healthy dose of each. Nobody can precisely balance equal amounts of all five elements at all times, but the closer we get to balancing our personality elements, the more effective and successful we'll be in all aspects of our lives. Here are some of the ways the balance of elements affects personality. These remedies, like all the remedies you'll find in this book, will be most effective when you reinforce them with the Three Secrets Reinforcement ritual, which we discuss in Lesson 12.

Fire
Too little: Unmotivated, can't express feelings

Too much: Emotionally volatile, judgmental

Balanced: Fair-minded, appropriately expressive

Earth
Too little: Selfish, insincere

Too much: Generous to a fault, self-sacrificing

Balanced: Appropriately nurturing, caring, reliable

Water
Too little: Limited knowledge, narrow-minded

Too much: Has much knowledge but can't use it well

Balanced: Intelligent, insightful, full of wisdom

Metal
Too little: Timid, unable to communicate

Too much: Motor-mouthed, "brassy," self-righteous

Balanced: Eloquent, conversationally adept

Wood
Too little: Ungrounded, easily influenced

Too much: Inflexible, stubborn

Balanced: Strongly principled but open-minded

To balance the elements in your personality, increase or decrease those that are imbalanced by adding or removing symbolic shapes, colors, and textures in your environment, clothing, and diet.

In addition to these adjustments, feng shui offers specific rituals to help you balance the elements in your personality.

student experience

"Now I understand why I have always had a sense of peace when I am with my brother. His birth star is earth and mine is water; our personalities complement each other. He has always been a calming presence in my life."
—Paul, landscaper

Whether you have too much or too little of an element, or you simply want to give yourself a "tune-up" to keep everything in balance, you can perform the following rituals:

Fire: In the morning, take one deep breath in, exhale in eight short breaths, then make the ninth exhalation a long one. Repeat this breathing exercise nine times. Do this for 27 days.

Earth: Place nine small stones in a *yu* bowl (an ancient porcelain ink bowl). Fill the bowl 70 percent with clear water and expose it to the sky. Place it in your bedroom. Every morning, change the water and expose it to the sky again. Do this for 27 days.

Water: To adjust your still water, place a small, round mirror under your mattress where your head rests. Wipe it clean each morning while imagining that your mind and thoughts are becoming clearer. Do this for 27 days. To adjust your moving water, meet, call, write, e-mail, or fax 9, 18, or 27 new people (or people you haven't been in touch with for 6 months) each day for 9, 18, or 27 consecutive days (any of these 3 numbers is effective; the main requirement is that the number of contacts and days be a multiple of 9). Don't complain or ask them for favors.

Metal: Place a nonmetal finger ring under your mattress for nine days, and then wear it on your middle finger for 27 days.

Wood: Obtain three healthy potted plants. Place one near your front door, one in your living room, and one in your bedroom. If any of them dies, replace it immediately with a healthier, more expensive one.

HOW FENG SHUI COMPLEMENTS AND ENHANCES DESTINY

According to ancient Chinese wisdom, we're very unlikely to succeed in life unless we're aware of our destiny. Destiny is the realm of tien chai, the one sphere we can't do anything to change. We can directly affect our ren chai through our choices, and can influence our ti chai. But our destiny was fixed at our birth and remains a constant throughout our lives.

a note from
the instructor

FIVE LIFE FACTORS THAT DETERMINE YOUR SUCCESS

- **Fate:** Your destiny, your natal chi energy—the sum total of your human potential
- **Luck:** Auspicious and inauspicious periods in your life
- **Feng shui:** The pattern of energy flow in your environment
- **Karma:** Your attitude, intentions, and deeds
- **Diligence:** Your efforts to cultivate your chi: hard work, education, self-improvement

Feng shui recognizes that, although we can't change our destiny, we can change our attitudes, behaviors, and environment to make the most of the destiny heaven has dealt us. To do this, we need to get the clearest possible picture of what our destiny is. Armed with this information, we can choose in advance how we'll respond to future events.

As we've just seen with the animal zodiac and the nine-star ki, feng shui touches upon, and relates to, many forms of astrology and divination. The Black Sect school of feng shui relies primarily on intuition and intuitive abilities, while the Compass school uses the Four Pillars of Destiny.

THE FOUR PILLARS OF DESTINY

Feng shui masters use the Four Pillars of Destiny to "map" an individual's tien chai (heaven luck) so that he or she may assess the impact of destiny on his or her life. The Four Pillars correspond to four time increments that mark an individual's birth: 1) year, 2) month, 3) day, and 4) hour.

Each pillar is further divided into "heavenly stems" and "earthly branches." The ten heavenly stems consist of yin and yang aspects of the five elements, for a total of ten possible values (yin fire, yang fire, yin earth, yang earth, and so forth).

The 12 earthly branches correspond to the 12 Chinese zodiac animals. Each pillar is expressed as an animal (its earthly branch), and each animal contains up to three yin or yang aspects of one of the five elements (stems). For example, if you were born in 1965, your year pillar identifies you as a yin wood snake (the Four Pillars method doesn't use the same system as the nine-star ki, so although your zodiac animal remains the same, your element may be different). The yin wood snake is different from a yang fire snake or a yin water snake. Each combination of animal and yin or yang stem contributes to a unique personality and destiny.

Your other three pillars also have an associated animal with a yin or yang element. The animals and elements of your year, month, day, and hour affect the different aspects of your personality and life potentials. Your day pillar, in particular the day heavenly stem, is considered to be the key to your personality and character: It reveals your true nature.

In addition to the personality traits we explored in the previous lesson, the Four Pillars can reveal information about potential health risks, favorable professions, auspicious investment times, and potential wealth and love opportunities. They reveal the patterns of luck flowing through your life, and can pinpoint lucky and unlucky phases in each year. They can also recommend the best careers, mates, and living arrangements, and put us on the lookout for possible hidden potentials. Since the process requires an elaborate chart and analysis, it's not possible to adequately cover the Four Pillars within the scope of this book. But if you're interested in learning more, read *The Treasures of Tao*, by David Twicken (Writers Club Press, 2002). If you're interested in a full interpretation of your Four Pillars chart, consult a qualified Chinese astrology expert.

CHOOSING CAREERS COMPATIBLE WITH YOUR DESTINY

According to the Four Pillars of Destiny, the best way to select a life's work is to become aware of the elemental characteristics of different types of businesses. You can then evaluate each potential career in terms of its suitability to your own elemental make-up, your strengths and weaknesses.

Often, the dominant element of your birth chart naturally draws you to career fields that also focus on that element. But this is not always the case. If you don't see yourself precisely in your birth day element, you may identify more strongly with one of the elements in your other three pillars. In this event, choose the fields that involve the element you need most to balance your chart. Focus on your weak element, and this will bring balance to your life.

Let's look at the five basic elemental personalities and the careers for which they're well suited. Rather than seeking a career in an element in which you're strong, you should seek a career associated with an element in which you're weak, to provide balance.

Fire: Fire people are lively and emotive. A person who is weak in fire will benefit from fire-related careers, such as performing arts, fashion, promotions, electrician, radiation technician, laser industries, air conditioning and heating, anything to do with firearms, baking, and fuel production.

Earth: Earth people are natural caretakers. Those weak in earth will do well in such earthy fields as medicine, food service, farming, ecology, and "homey" ones like construction and real estate. They may benefit from careers as morticians and cemetery managers.

Water: Your choice of water-related careers depends largely on whether the type of water you're lacking is still or moving. Still water, because of its wise, reflective nature, is the element of teachers, professors, researchers, scholars, and mystics. Flowing water, with its connection to networking and communications, makes a good match with most of the health care professions. Any profession that contains some sort of "flow" may prove satisfying for those who need moving water: communications, transportation, teaching, and tourism.

Metal: Individuals who need more metal would do well in science, technology, blacksmithing, welding, automobile manufacture, engineering, the arts, sculpting, making metal jewelry or furniture, or designing software.

Wood: Since wood relates naturally to growth, individuals who need wood will benefit from such wood fields as teaching, gardening, law, religion, politics, and literature. They also do well in fields that use wood or plant materials: lumber, furniture, textiles, and paper products.

a note from
the instructor

FENG SHUI CAREER FINDER

The time of year in which you were born is also associated with an element. If your birth year element fails to match you with a career that feels right, your season element may be more important in determining your ideal work, provided that it's the element you need to bring balance to your life. Consult a Chinese astrology expert for more details.

If You Were Born In...	You May Be Highly...	So Consider a Career In...
Spring (February–April)	Wood	Writing, education, construction
Summer (May–July)	Fire	Entertainment, arts, fashion
Harvest (July)	Earth	Food service, health care
Autumn (August–October)	Metal	Planning, computers, engineering
Winter (November–January)	Water	Teaching, tourism, transportation

CHOOSING RELATIONSHIPS COMPATIBLE WITH YOUR DESTINY

Typically, partners will react to each other in ways that are true to their element. Relationships in which one partner's element nourishes the other's—provided that the other's does the first no harm—generally work well. But where one partner's element damages or strongly controls the other, the consequences can be dire. But if the controlling element isn't too powerful, it may have a beneficial "tempering effect."

Beneficial combinations: The following partnerships are likely to prove compatible (one element nurtures another): water with wood, wood with fire, fire with earth, earth with metal, metal with water.

Harmful combinations: Because of the harmful interaction of their elements, these partnerships could spell trouble: fire with water (think of volatile steam), metal with wood (the wood partner will be depleted), water with earth (the water partner will feel trapped and "clogged").

These pairings might work: If an individual has an extreme excess of his or her dominant element, he or she may find it helpful to choose a partner who "controls" that element. A little fire tempers hard metal; a small amount of metal prunes wood; a few burrowing wooden roots could stir up earth that has become too settled.

Good and bad marriage material: Some elemental personalities make for better marriage partners than others. Earth people tend to be stable and loving mates—if not terribly stimulating. Wood people also make loyal, trustworthy spouses, although they can be somewhat inflexible.

Fire people, if their element is too intense, may not be able to share their own "light," and others may find their volatility too challenging to consider matrimony. If their element is well balanced, they may prove to be lively, fun, passionate partners.

Metal people can be extremely fascinating or extremely irritating mates. They can sometimes seem cold, and they're perhaps a little *too* skilled in argument. They can become too preoccupied to provide loving attention; on the other hand, they can offer a lifetime of stimulating conversation.

Water people, if their element is active, may be difficult to get close to. They can be changeable and restless. But their social sphere is almost always a lively one. Still water people make for calm, wise mates, but it's difficult to convince them to go out on a Saturday night.

FENG SHUI LESSON-END QUESTIONS

Lesson #11:

1. With which (one or more) of the five elements do you identify most closely?

_____

_____

_____

2. Which elements in your personality could use adjustment? Do these elements need to be strengthened or toned down?

_____

_____

_____

3. Does your career challenge you to develop the element(s) in which you're weak, or does it tap into one(s) in which you're already strong?

_____

_____

_____

4. If you're in a relationship, describe the strong and weak elements in your partner. How would you characterize the interaction of the elements between the two of you?

_____

_____

_____

5. If you're seeking a relationship, what elements in a potential mate would help you balance those in your own personality? What strengths, elementally speaking, do you have to offer a partner?

_____

_____

_____

6. With which (one or more) of the Chinese Zodiac animals do you identify most closely? (Note: The animal that seems to fit you best might not be the one of your birth year.)

_____

_____

_____

7. If you're in a relationship, which Chinese Zodiac animal typi-
fies your mate? Are your animal and your mate's animal compatible? Describe the way their interaction manifests in your
relationship.

_____

_____

_____

Other Thoughts:

_____

_____

_____

_____

_____

_____

feng shui and the power of intention

The Mind/Body Connection • Mundane and Transcendental Feng Shui • Three Secrets of Reinforcement • Intention and Visualization • Feng Shui Ceremonies

We've saved the most powerful feng shui for last. In the first nine lessons, you learned how to arrange your environment to enhance your goals and opportunities; in the tenth and eleventh lessons, you discovered how to recognize the roles that personality and destiny play in the choices you make. Now we want to offer you a tool that will greatly enhance every other feng shui teaching you've absorbed.

As we've discussed, your feng shui efforts will meet with a certain amount of success, even if you don't believe in them, and even if your thoughts are elsewhere as you perform your feng shui enhancements and remedies. But what we're about to show you will dramatically increase the effectiveness of any feng shui you do.

You're about to add the power of *intention* to your feng shui.

Intention is desire, motivation, the willful choosing of a goal. It's what takes place in your mind and spirit before you take that first physical action. In spiritual terms, it's the act of launching the chi of your desires into the universe. It's synonymous with will, passion, and mission, and it works like rocket fuel on your feng shui efforts.

For example, if you simply perform a few enhancements in your Career area without giving any thought to what you hope to achieve (paint your door red, bury nine Chinese coins outside the entry, add a flowing fountain), you'll probably experience some improvement in your work life. But if you clearly pinpoint a desired career goal (a promotion, authorship of a book, etc.), visualize your success vividly, and throw all your passion behind it, then it's a safe bet your red door, Chinese coins, and flowing fountain will be far more effective.

In this lesson, we'll explain the background behind this teaching. Then we'll introduce you to a magnificent ritual, the Three Secrets Reinforcement, which will help you put your intentions into motion.

INTENTION AND FORM: THE MIND/BODY CONNECTION

How does intention work? The Black Sect school of feng shui teaches that whatever we hold in our minds can become manifest in the physical world. If we send forth our mental chi with focus and determination, it can reverberate within the chi of the universe to help bring about the result we intend.

To make the power of intention work for you, you don't need to be a Buddhist, a Taoist, or a mystic. You only need to recognize that *anything is possible*. The energy of the universe is malleable and flowing—in a constant state of change. We can act upon the universe to affect the way it changes—or at least, to affect the way our corner of it changes. If you believe in the possibility of change, you can make intention work for you.

MUNDANE AND TRANSCENDENTAL FENG SHUI

The Black Sect school operates on two distinct levels: *sying*, or tangible elements, and *yi*, the intangible. Sying is the mundane, practical, logical realm of feng shui, which seeks to raise your energy level by cleaning, repairing, and de-cluttering your home, and filling it with energizing colors, lights, and plants.

But beyond these "earthbound" adjustments to the material world lies the realm of yi, the transcendental, spiritual, and illogical. We can build no absolute scientific evidence to explain why certain yi remedies and rituals are so effective, because science, by its nature, can deal only with the physical, observable world. Yet for reasons we may never grasp, *they work*.

In fact, it's a core belief of the Black Sect that the illogical solutions work much better than the logical ones. It even suggests that we all operate from illogical, unscientific data far more often than we realize. We live the vast majority of our lives on intuitive guesswork, and on our faith in things that we can't quantify.

If you have read the previous chapters of this book, you now have a good understanding of the way feng shui works in the realm of sying. Now let's add the powerful, transcendental yi of intention to your feng shui efforts.

 a note from the instructor

THE GREAT SUNSHINE BUDDHA MEDITATION

This simple meditation technique cleanses and recharges your chi. You'll also derive great benefit from practicing this meditation regularly, and any time you need an energy boost:

Step 1 Stand comfortably and turn your face up to the sun; hold out your hands, palms upward. Imagine the energy of the sun flowing into your body through the palms of your hands and through the "third eye" at the sixth *chakra* in the center of your forehead (this is the center for wisdom, dreams, imagination, and spiritual vision).

Feel it filling your whole body with the radiant energy of the sunshine. The light then exits from the soles of your feet. Lower your arms.

Step 2 Repeat this meditation while visualizing the sunshine traveling all the way down to the bottom of your feet, then quickly upward and out through your palms and third eye. Lower your arms.

Step 3 On the third repetition, imagine the energy reaching the soles of your feet, deliberately and gradually moving upward, swirling gently through all your limbs and organs, removing all your pain and sickness, before flowing out again through your palms and third eye.

THREE SECRETS REINFORCEMENT

The Three Secrets Reinforcement ritual uses three powerful sources of chi to enhance your feng shui efforts: your body, your speech, and your mind. When you perform this ritual, you're moving your intentions into the universe, starting them on their journey to materialization. This ritual is most effective when performed just before you undertake any feng shui enhancements or remedies.

Before beginning the Three Secrets Reinforcement ritual, or any other ritual, it is important that you meditate. Meditation enables you to calm yourself, clear your mind, and prepare your chi to connect with that of the universe. One excellent meditation aid is the Calming Heart Mantra (spiritual chant). This mantra can be done anywhere and at any time to calm your own chi, whether or not you're performing a feng shui adjustment. To use it, stand or sit comfortably and repeat the following syllables nine times:

Gate, gaté,

Para gaté,

Para sum gaté,

Bodhi svaha.

To strengthen your mantra, you may add a *mudra*, or spiritual gesture. The Heart and Mind Calming Mudra works well in this context: While sitting or standing comfortably, touch the tips of your thumbs together with your palms facing upward. Rest your left hand on your right in a relaxed circle.

You may also use the praying gesture (two upright palms pressed together) to get yourself into a peaceful attitude.

Now you're ready to perform the Three Secrets Reinforcement. Perform all three simultaneously at the site that requires the adjustment, at the same time that you do the following feng shui enhancements.

Body

Put your bodily energy into your intention by performing a mudra suitable to the occasion. Try the Expelling Mudra for clearing harmful chi: With your index and pinkie fingers raised, flick your middle and ring fingers outward against your thumb repeatedly.

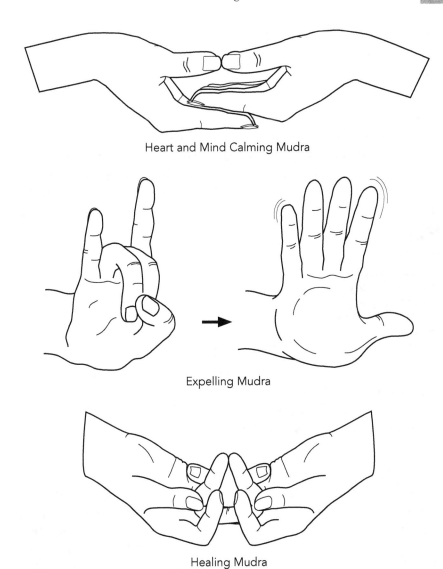

Heart and Mind Calming Mudra

Expelling Mudra

Healing Mudra

Three mudras.

Speech

Chant a mantra to put the energy of the spoken word into your intention. I recommend the powerful Six True Syllables Mantra:

Om Ma Ni Pad Me Hum

You may use this, or any mantra that works best for you. Or you may recite a prayer or other form of spiritual speech from your own religious tradition.

Mind

This is the most vital of the three secrets. As you're chanting and performing your mudra, hold a clear image of your goal in your mind. Form a clear picture of what your life will be like when your goal is achieved. Use sight, sound, and emotion.

student experience

"I performed the ritual on Easter Sunday. It felt very empowering, and the next day I was able to break through some career obstacles. Thanks so much for all your input."

—Jerry, electrical engineer

Give your visualization as much detail as you can. Feel what it will be like to have your intention become reality.

How often should you perform this ritual? You need to do it only once for each adjustment, but you may repeat it if you feel that your previous visualization wasn't sufficient. When you perform the ritual, do it with all focus and sincerity, then trust that the process is under way.

When to Perform Your Ritual

Perform your ritual just before you undertake any feng shui adjustments or enhancements. Any time of day works, but the hours between 11:00 A.M. and 1:00 P.M., and between 11:00 P.M. and 1:00 A.M. are the most auspicious, because this is when day turns to night and night turns to day. These times are full of their own transformative energy. Since the universe is already in motion during these hours, your intentions will take advantage of this natural momentum.

What to Do After You've Performed Your Ritual

Now that you've performed your enhancements and strengthened them with your intention and visualization, it's time to sit back and wait quietly. However excited you may be, resist the urge to talk about your ritual and the enhancements or remedies you've done. Discussing them leaks energy from your intentions.

Be patient. Don't wait in a constant state of anxiety for your intentions to be fulfilled. Go about your life secure in the knowledge that your intentions are "out there" and that the universe has "heard" you. The universe works on its own timetable, so it may not be today, or next week, or even next month, but trust that it will happen at the proper time.

Anticipate, with calm assurance, that the universe will answer your intention, although the answer may not necessarily come in the form you expect. Remember that whatever you send out comes back to you. Keep your chi calm, uplifted, and full of hope.

Good things are on their way.

FENG SHUI BLESSING CEREMONIES

The Three Secrets Reinforcement we just discussed will greatly strengthen any of your feng shui efforts, from simple adjustments around your home to more elaborate ceremonies. In this section we'll offer a few common feng shui blessing ceremonies. The power of each of these ceremonies is greatly enhanced when you combine it with intention and visualization.

The Rice Blessing

This is a traditional Chinese blessing used to cleanse and purify a new home or business, but it can also be used to clear away the negative chi of unfortunate events. This blessing is traditionally performed outdoors, but if you live in an apartment or townhouse, you can do this indoors; just try to leave the rice where it falls for at least 24 hours.

1. Begin by calming yourself with the Heart and Mind Calming Mantra, or another mantra or prayer of your choice.

2. In a large bowl, mix five to eight pounds of uncooked rice with cinnabar powder and several drops (one drop for each year of your age plus one) of liquor, 80-proof or stronger. Use your middle finger to stir the mixture—your left hand if you're female, your right hand if you're male.

3. Repeat the Buddha's Six True Syllables Mantra (Om Ma Ni Pad Me Hum) or the mantra/prayer of your choice 108 times.

4. At your front door, do the following:

Throw a handful of rice straight up in the air, repeating the Buddha's Six True Syllables Mantra (to uplift the chi).

Toss one handful outward, repeating the Buddha's Six True Syllables Mantra (to "feed" and appease harmful forces).

Toss a handful straight down, repeating the Buddha's Six True Syllables Mantra (to symbolize sowing the seeds of a new beginning).

5. Walk around your property, stopping to repeat this ritual wherever you feel it's necessary (let your intuition guide you).

6. Perform the intention and visualization, as discussed earlier in this lesson.

The Orange Peel Purification

This simple ritual is a great way to clear the air of negative chi. Float the skins of nine oranges in a bowl. Dip your fingers in the water and sprinkle it liberally all around your home. Perform the Three Secrets Reinforcement.

Sealing the Door

This ritual guards your home against the intrusion of negative energies and bad luck. In a small bowl, combine cinnabar powder and liquor: one drop of liquor for every year of your age plus one. Dip your finger in the mixture and touch your front door from the inside on the top and sides. Do this on all the other exterior doors—even garage doors. Mix the remaining solution with water and pour it down all drains to symbolically seal them, including sinks and toilets. Then perform the Three Secrets Reinforcement.

The Red Cloth Travel Remedy

To attract good chi to your travels, or to a new stage of your life (such as marriage or promotion), spread a six-foot-long section of red cloth through your front doorway, with three feet on one side and three feet on the other. Walk through the doorway over the cloth and imagine yourself having a pleasant, safe journey (or transition). Then perform the Three Secrets Reinforcement.

appendix a

sources and suggested reading

Brown, Simon. *Feng Shui in a Weekend*. New York: Hamlyn Publishing Co., 2001.

—. *Feng Shui Solutions*. London: Cassell & Co., 2000.

Chiazzari, Suzy. *Home Harmony: Using the Five Elements to Create a Blissful, Balanced Home*. North Pomfret, VT: Trafalgar Square Publishing, 2001.

Chin, R. D. *Feng Shui Revealed: An Aesthetic, Practical Approach to the Ancient Art of Space Alignment*. Clarkson N. Potter, 1998.

Chuen, Lam Kam. *The Personal Feng Shui Manual: How to Develop a Healthy and Harmonious Lifestyle*. New York: Henry Holt & Co., 1998.

Jones, Katina Z. *The Everything Feng Shui Book: Create Harmony and Peace in Any Room*. Avin, MA: Adams Media Corporation, 2002.

Kennedy, David Daniel. *Feng Shui for Dummies*. Indianapolis, IN: Wiley Publishing, Inc., 2001.

Kingston, Karen. *Clear Your Clutter with Feng Shui*. New York: Broadway Books, 1999.

Linn, Denise. *Feng Shui for the Soul: How to Create a Harmonious Environment That Will Nurture and Sustain You*. Carlsbad, CA: Hay House, 2000.

Moran, Elizabeth, and Val Biktashev. *The Complete Idiot's Guide to Feng Shui*. New York: Alpha Books, 1999.

Pitchford, Paul. *Healing with Whole Foods: Oriental Traditions and Modern Nutrition*. Berkeley, CA: North Atlantic Books, 2002.

Post, Steven. *The Modern Book of Feng Shui: Vitality and Harmony for the Home and Office*. New York: Dell Publishing Co., 1998.

Rossbach, Sarah. *Interior Design with Feng Shui*. New York: Penguin Books, 2000.

Rossbach, Sarah, and Master Lin Yun. *Living Color: Master Lin Yun's Guide to Feng Shui and the Art of Color*. New York: Kodansha International, 1994.

Sandifer, Jon. *Feng Shui Astrology*. New York: Ballantine Books, 1997.

—. *Feng Shui and Health*. New York: Three Rivers Press, 2002.

SantoPietro, Nancy. *Feng Shui: Harmony by Design*. Berkeley, CA: Berkeley Publishing Group, 1996.

Sung, Edgar. *The 10,000 Years Book*. San Francisco: M. J. E. Publishing, 2003.

Too, Lillian. *The Illustrated Encyclopedia of Feng Shui*. Boston: Element Books Ltd., 1999.

Twicken, David. *Classical Five Element Chinese Astrology Made Easy*. Writers Club Press, 2000.

—. *Treasures of Tao*. Writers Club Press, 2002.

Wong, Eva. *Feng Shui: The Ancient Wisdom of Harmonious Living for Modern Times*. Boston: Shambhala Publications, 1996.

—. *A Master Course in Feng Shui*. Boston: Shambhala Publications, 2001.

Wydra, Nancilee. *Feng Shui Principles for Building and Remodeling*. New York: McGraw-Hill, 2002.

Yoshikawa, Takashi. *Feng Shui Astrology*. York Beach, ME: Samuel Weiser Inc., 1999.

feng shui and clothing

Like your home, your clothing is a symbolic extension of your body. It can affect not only your own chi but also the chi of the people around you. Your clothing has this effect whether you're aware of it or not, so the best thing you can do for yourself and those around you is to choose your attire consciously.

Choose clothing that harmonizes with the chi of that day's activity; for instance, if you're meeting with your banker, you might choose to wear wealth colors of green or purple. You may also choose colors that can help you with the particular goals you're trying to achieve. For instance, you might choose to add a white blouse to a particular outfit to avail yourself of the communicative powers of metal.

Several different aspects of clothing can affect chi: color, texture, pattern, style, and material. A blouse of soft, flannel-like material in a dove gray exudes a gentle yin chi, where a shiny silk blouse of vibrant red is extremely yang. Match the overall chi of the outfit to either the event or atmosphere of the day, or to the type of energy you wish to cultivate.

In general, let your intuition be your guide. Wear what you feel like wearing. However, don't wear the same colors every day, or you won't be able to keep your chi balanced. All dark colors could lead to depression;

all bright ones could cause tension and fatigue. Since your chi changes each day, you can't satisfy its needs with a limited selection of colors. Aim for a broad spectrum of colors and shades in your wardrobe.

CLOTHING STYLES

The style of clothing you choose to wear affects your chi by generating certain types of energy. It doesn't matter to your chi whether or not you're in fashion. What matters most is the type of lines that your clothing style creates. Severe lines, pleats, and piping create predominantly yang energy. Soft, billowy styles are predominantly yin. A military-inspired jacket is very yang, a peasant blouse very yin.

CLOTHING TEXTURES AND MATERIAL

In general, natural materials attract better chi than synthetics. Cotton, linen, silk, and wool (and blends that are predominantly made up of them) are preferable to 100% nylon or polyester.

Shiny textures, such as certain silks, are generally yang. Wear them to boost energy and attract attention. Soft, flannel-like textures are yin and inviting. Wearing them creates a low-key, soothing effect. Course fabric textures (as some wools and linens have) may be jarring and irritating to you and those around you.

CLOTHING COLORS

Colors carry multiple layers of symbolism in Chinese culture. Colors can be applied in many ways to influence mood and focus. The colors you choose to wear can have a profound effect on your mood and on the way you're perceived:

- **Red** is the traditional Chinese color of luck, wealth, happiness, fame, and strength. In a bygone era, nearly all Chinese brides wore this color. Red is directly associated with the Fame area of the ba-gua. Wear red when you want to enhance your reputation and get noticed, and wear it when you're seeking to augment your good fortune.

- **Green** is the color of growth, kindness, and hope. It's beneficial to wear green at beginnings — wear it when you're embarking on a new venture or entering a new stage of development. Green is also helpful in matters of health.

- **Black** is associated with still water, the color of deep wisdom. It may be beneficial to wear black when you're seeking wisdom or when you wish to appear wise. Black can also sometimes represent hopelessness, so wear it with caution.

- **Blue** is the color of moving water, of transactions and socializing, and of self-knowledge. It's also a secondary color of growth and wisdom. Wearing blue can assist your networking efforts.

- **Yellow** is associated with the earthy qualities of patience and nurture. Wearing yellow may assist you in public relations and in any scenario in which you're in a care-taking role. Yellow is also the color of happiness and stability, and it is often associated with royalty and emperors.

- **Brown** speaks of stability and maturity. It, too, is strongly associated with earth. Wear brown when you want to appear solid, stable, and settled.

- **Gray** is strongly associated with metal and the Helpful Friends area of the ba-gua. It can help you gain trustworthy allies and express your ideas clearly. It's also associated with righteousness.

- **White** is also associated with metal. It has strong associations with precision and decision-making. In Chinese culture, white is the primary color of mourning.

- **Purple** is the color of wealth and nobility. It's associated with power and charisma. Wear it when you want to get noticed.

- **Orange** is associated with happiness, power, and prosperity. The person wearing orange commands attention and respect.

- **Aqua** speaks of spring and beginnings. Wear this color at the start of a new venture.

- **Pink** strongly symbolizes romance. This is the best color to wear if you wish to attract love. Pink is a traditional color for the Marriage area of the ba-gua, and it is also associated with motherhood.

CLOTHING PRINTS AND PATTERNS

In Chinese culture, patterns and motifs carry powerful meanings just as colors do. For instance, a dragon image on your clothing can be extremely auspicious. Many traditional feng shui masters wore clothing embroidered with dragons so that they could enjoy its protection as they worked. The Chinese Zodiac animals (rat, ox, tiger, rabbit, dragon, snake, horse, sheep, rooster, monkey, dog, and pig) are generally auspicious images to wear, especially if you choose images of your own animal.

The patterns you choose may also affect your chi and the chi of those around you. Angular, geometric clothing patterns exude yang energy. Soft, flowing lines and shapes, and very small patterns are mostly yin.

feng shui and food

The impact food has on our senses is far more profound than we realize; it affects our chi in many of the same ways that our surroundings and clothing do. You tend to eat more and get more enjoyment from your food when it's appetizing and arranged in a pleasing manner. Dieters are satisfied with less food if that food is served in a way that appears bountiful and overflowing — even if it's a smaller portion. The taste, texture, and amount of food are only part of what makes it satisfying; a large part of the experience is also its color. Because colorful food stimulates us more, it's more satisfying.

Because of the effect it has on our chi, the color of our food can also affect our health. You may remember that in Lesson 2 we discussed the various layers of meaning associated with the five elements; remember that each element is associated with a vital organ. The same tradition that spawned feng shui advises that if you need to improve the health of a particular organ, you should eat the foods that are associated with its element.

Below you'll find several of the body's primary organs, the elements with which they're associated, and the foods that are strong in that particular element. Remember, though, that you won't be able to cure a serious health problem simply by eating these foods. If you're receiving proper medical care, these foods may assist your healing, but they're not cures in and of themselves.

- **The liver** is associated with the element wood. To improve liver health, eat bright green foods such as peas, celery, cabbage, and spinach.

- **The heart** is associated with fire. To stimulate heart health, enjoy tomatoes, red peppers, shrimp, and lobster.

- **The stomach** is associated with earth. To improve digestive health, eat yellow squash, carrots, and eggs.

- **The lungs** are associated with metal. Boost your intake of fish, chicken, scallops, and egg whites to aid your lungs.

- **The kidneys** are naturally associated with water. To improve your kidneys' health, eat black beans, beef, and eggplant.

appendix d

palm reading

According to the Black Hat Sect school of feng shui (and other teachings), the palms of our hands contain detailed diagrams of our lives. We can learn a great deal about our fates, our changes in fortune, our health, wealth, careers, family life, and our relationships by studying our palms. Of particular importance are the lines, marks, colors, and patterns on our palms.

Whereas some forms of palm reading (even that of traditional Chinese Palmistry) use the palm of only one hand, the Black Hat Sect uses the palms and fingers of both hands. One hand reveals the destiny that was given you on the day that you were born; the other shows the influences that have affected your destiny *since* your birth.

For women, the right hand shows the original fate, and the left hand shows the alterations. On men, the left hand shows the original stamp of destiny, and the right hand shows the changes.

A Black Hat Sect palm reading begins with a reading of the pre-natal hand, the one that reveals your original destiny. The palm reader then compares these lines with those of the post-natal hand.

When looking at your palms, begin with your life line. This line runs diagonally from the top of your palm near the base of the pointer finger, down toward the center of the heel of your hand. If the line is broken, feathered, or indistinct at any point, this could indicate impending illnesses or accidents.

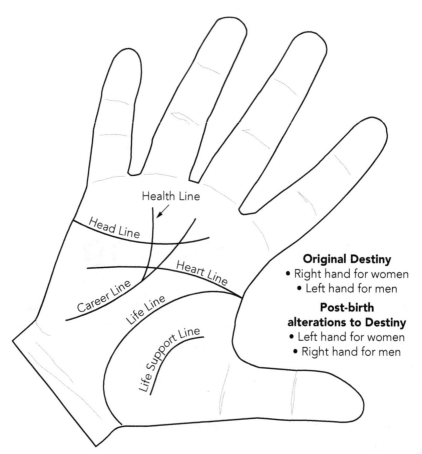

Black Hat Sect palm reading.

Next, look at your heart line. This line runs horizontally from the outside of your palm to the center. If this is solid and distinct, your emotional life will be a smooth one. If it branches out, your love life will be marked with affairs.

Your life support line runs parallel to your life line, lying between the life line and thumb. If this line is strong — particularly in places where the life line is faint or broken — you'll have help during difficult times.

The career line runs vertically along the center of your palm. Read this line from the bottom up. A solid single line indicates a rewarding career. Any break in the line could indicate a change in careers.

Last but not least, your health line branches off at an angle from the career line. A distinct, solid line indicates a lifetime of good health; breaks in the line foretell potential health problems.

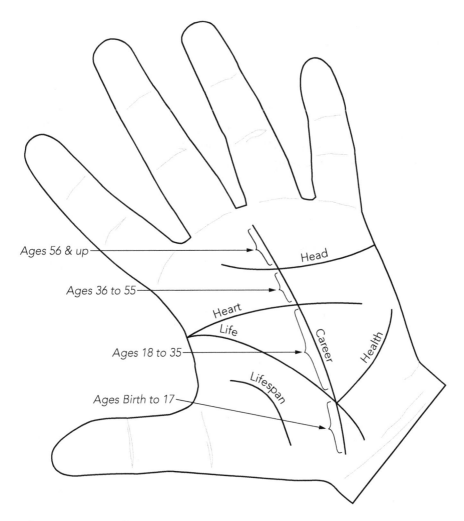

Life stages on your palm.

Your palm can also give you clues to what age you will be when certain events happen. You'll know when to expect major changes in your career by reading your career line in relation to its intersection with your heart line. The part of the line that runs below the heart line traces your career up to your 35th birthday. The part that runs between the heart line and the head line (the uppermost horizontal line) shows developments in your career when you're between the ages of 36 and 55. The portion above the head line indicates events after the age of 55.

BTB palmistry also places the ba-gua on your palm. The career area sits at the heel of your hand, knowledge at the base of your thumb, fame at the base of your middle finger, and so forth. BTB palm readers often press parts of the palm and read the colors that appear to tell the relative strength or weakness of that area in the individual's life.

The fingers of your hand represent the important people in your life. Your middle finger represents you, your ring finger symbolizes your spouse and friends, your thumb stands for your parents, your pointer finger your siblings, and your pinkie your children. Asymmetrical marks, indentations, or discolorations on any given finger can indicate troubles with the relationship that finger represents.

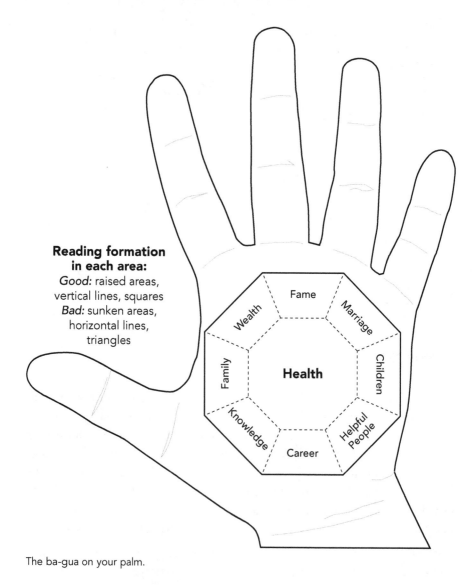

Reading formation in each area:
Good: raised areas, vertical lines, squares
Bad: sunken areas, horizontal lines, triangles

Fame
Wealth
Marriage
Family
Health
Children
Knowledge
Career
Helpful People

The ba-gua on your palm.

Each finger also represents one of the five elements: wood (green) for the thumb, fire (red) for the pointer, earth (yellow/brown) for the middle finger, metal (white) for the ring finger, and water (blue/black) for the pinkie. When you're having difficulties with someone from one of these groups, wear a ring the color of that particular element on the corresponding finger. For instance, if you've had a falling-out with your spouse and are trying to mend fences, wearing a white ring on your ring finger may assist your efforts.

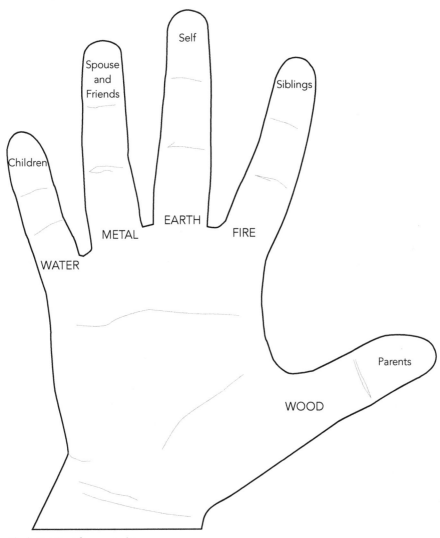

Black Hat Sect finger reading.

appendix e

feng shui for travelers

Travel can have a profound effect on our chi. We make ourselves extremely vulnerable when we travel — we're exposed to a vast array of influences, many of which we can't control. Feng shui teaches that we need special protection at such times.

Feng shui considers you to be traveling not only when you take a long trip away from home, but also any time you must leave your house — for instance, when you're commuting to work or running errands. Travel is any journey that takes you out of your normal environment and exposes you to the unpredictable chi of the outside world.

Do what you can to protect your chi from disruptive influences when you travel. Start out on a positive note with your chi in the right place, and prepare to "refresh" your chi at regular intervals with rest and positive visualization. Before and during your travel, take time to imagine yourself arriving safely at your destination and returning safely home. While traveling, do daily exercises (like the Great Sunshine Buddha Meditation discussed in Lesson 12) to keep your chi calm, balanced, and healthy.

When you're staying in a hotel, apply the same principles as you would at your home or office. If you have the choice, pick a room that's away from stairwells, elevator shafts, and busy thoroughfares. Surround yourself with your four guardians when you sleep. Bring your favorite objects from home, and create a symbolic altar to make you feel more "homey" and secure while traveling.

The helpful people area of the ba-gua is also the travel area. Use the same colors, shapes, and imagery to minister to your travels as you do to minister to this area. Wear gray and white clothing with metal accessories, particularly in sphere and dome shapes, if you wish to activate your travel opportunities.

feng shui colors for your business

Because color has such a profound affect on our chi and on the chi of those around us, it makes sense that you take care when choosing the colors for your business environment. The colors you present in your logo, on the walls of your establishment, in your furniture, décor, and products will greatly influence the way you are perceived.

By now you're familiar with much of the symbolism behind colors. You know what's auspicious, and you can choose the colors that enhance the impression you wish to make. What follows are a few suggestions for auspicious color schemes for several types of businesses. None of these are obligatory, of course, but you may find them helpful:

- **Accounting/Financial Business (white and yellow):** White symbolizes precision, yellow stability. Both colors symbolize metal (gold and silver) and, by extension, money.

- **Book Shop (blue, green, and yellow):** Blue is associated with knowledge (as well as trust), green with growth, and yellow with stability.

- **Clothing Store, Men's (blue and gray):** Blue represents knowledge and transaction; gray represents communication.

- **Clothing Store, Women's (blue and green):** Blue represents knowledge and transaction; green represents growth and principle.

- **Computer-Related Business (green, black, and yellow):** Green indicates growth, black symbolizes wisdom, and yellow symbolizes stability.

- **Law Office (black, white, gray, blue, and yellow):** Black exudes wisdom, white is associated with precision and communication, gray is associated with helpful allies and communication, blue is associated with trust and knowledge, and yellow symbolizes stability.

- **Medical Office (blue, green, white, and pink):** Blue and green stand for growth, white assists communication and precision, and pink symbolizes love and nurturance.

- **Restaurants (yellow, green, and pink or red):** Yellow symbolizes trust and nurturing qualities; green is not only lucky, but it also symbolizes freshness; and pink or red stimulates the appetite.

for aspiring feng shui professionals

If you feel that your initial interest in feng shui may be calling you deeper, and you're considering a career in feng shui, you may want to contact the following organizations for more information and training:

- **The Boston School of Feng Shui**

  781-643-2758

  www.lasassociates.com

- **BTB Feng Shui Professional Training Program**

  www.btbfengshui.com

- **Feng Shui Alliance**

  201-941-0259

  www.fengshuialliance.com

- **Feng Shui Research Center**

  www.astro-fengshui.com

- **Lin Yun Temple**

  510-841-2347

  www.yunlintemple.org

- **Long Island Feng Shui Institute**

  516-621-9898

  www.fengshuischools.com

- **Mindfulness Intention Feng Shui**

  215-546-0488

  www.MelaniLewandowski.com

- **The New England School of Feng Shui**

  203-268-9483, 203-272-3765

  www.neschoolfengshui.com

glossary of feng shui terms

ba-gua (BAH-gwah): The octagonal "relative compass" favored by the Black Hat Sect school of feng shui, which recognizes eight aspirations of life that correspond to specific ba-gua directions: Career at bottom center, Knowledge at bottom left, Family at center left, Wealth at top left, Fame at top center, Marriage at top right, Children at center right, Helpful People at bottom right, and overall health at the center (the tai chi). The ba-gua orients a home or workplace relative to its front door.

Black Hat sect feng shui (also known as the Black Sect Tantric Buddhism, or BTB, feng shui): The most popular school of feng shui in the United States, the Black Hat Sect school was founded in 1974 by H. H. Grandmaster Professor Thomas Lin-Yun. It incorporates the essence of Confucianism, Taoism, yin-yang philosophy, eclecticism, esoteric Buddhism, *I Ching*, the theory of chi, holistic healing, feng shui, and folkloric studies. Instead of using lo pan compass directions, the largely intuitive Black Hat Sect method uses the ba-gua and the "mouth of chi" to determine which areas of a home or workplace represent the eight aspirations of life.

black tortoise: One of the four *landform guardians* that protect a home or other site. The tortoise, the most important of the four, is located at the back of the site. It appears as a solid hill, mountain, or hump of trees. It is associated with winter, with warriors (as in benevolent protection), and with longevity.

Blessing Mudra (MUH-drah): A spiritual gesture, performed to bestow the blessing of good chi. With palms up, cross both pinkies and both middle fingers, hold the pinkies down with the thumbs in a pair of circles, hold the middle fingers down with the index fingers, and allow the ring fingers to stand upright back to back.

Buddhism: A major religion that originated in India with its founder Siddhartha Gautama (566 BC–486 BC). Buddhism spread to China during the Han Dynasty (206 BC–220 AD), but is not directly related to feng shui. Its primary association with feng shui is a modern one, through BTB feng shui founder Grandmaster Professor Thomas Lin-Yun.

Calming Heart Mantra (MAHN-trah): Also known as the Heart and Mind Calming Mantra. Recited at the beginning of any feng shui ritual of intention to calm the mind. Its syllables are "Gaté, gaté, para gaté, para sam gaté, Bodhi svaha."

chakras (CHAH-krahs): The portals in the body through which chi enters and exits. The most important of these is located at the top of the head. See also *meridians*.

chi (CHEE): The energy that flows from and through all living things; the vitality; the breath; also called "the dragon's cosmic breath." It is also the invisible energy that links everything living and nonliving. Chi may be beneficial or harmful. Contrast this term with tao, the raw force of the universe.

chi kung (chee-KOONG): A martial art that teaches participants to train and channel their chi for better health and strength.

Chinese 12-animal zodiac: The Chinese system of 12 animals (rat, ox, tiger, rabbit, dragon, snake, horse, sheep, monkey, rooster, dog, and pig), each with distinct traits, strengths, and weaknesses, each of which represents a year. In the Four Pillars Chinese astrology, each animal also represents a month, a day, and a 2-hour segment of a 24-hour cycle. Each is also associated with an element.

command position: The most powerful location and orientation in any given room. An individual sitting or sleeping in the command position has a full view of the door but is not directly in line with it. His or her back is against a solid object, such as a wall, without a window or doorway directly behind.

Compass feng shui: The basis of numerous schools of feng shui, Compass feng shui recognizes specific types of energies in the directions of the compass, as determined by the lo pan.

Confucianism: A major religion founded by the philosopher Confucius, who lived from 551 BC to 479 BC. Confucianism laid much of the groundwork for the development of feng shui.

dog: One of the 12 Chinese zodiac animals, associated with the element earth and the hours of 7:00 P.M. to 9:00 P.M. The most recent dog year was 1994.

dragon: One of the 12 Chinese zodiac animals, associated with the element earth and the hours of 7:00 A.M. to 9:00 A.M. The most recent dragon year was 2000.

earth: One of the five elements. Earth is stable and nurturing. It is associated with health, and with yellows and earth tones.

Expelling Mudra (MUH-drah): A spiritual gesture, performed to banish harmful chi and clear the way for change. With the index and pinkie fingers raised, the middle and ring finger are flicked repeatedly against the thumb.

fire: One of the five elements. Fire is inflaming, igniting, and uplifting. Fire is associated with summer, with reputation and passion, and with the color red.

five elements: The study of the unique energies and interactions of the five essential elements of feng shui: fire, earth, metal, water, wood.

Form school: Sometimes called the Landform school, Form school feng shui is the oldest feng shui teaching. It examines the landscape of a given area to determine the most auspicious building locations.

green dragon: One of the four landform guardians that protect a home or other site. It appears in the landscape as a line of gently undulating hills, trees, or shrubs. The dragon is located to the left of the site from the aspect of the front door. It is associated with springtime, with luck, and with the positive flow of wealth.

Heart and Mind Calming Mudra (MUH-drah): A spiritual gesture to calm the heart and mind. While touching the tips of both thumbs together, cradle the left hand in the right to form a relaxed circle. This mudra is typically performed while reciting the Calming Heart Mantra.

horse: One of the 12 Chinese zodiac animals, associated with the element fire and the hours of 11:00 A.M. to 1:00 P.M. The most recent horse year was 2002.

I Ching: The ancient cosmological text from which such feng shui principles as the ba-gua and the Compass school draw their principles.

landform guardians: The four mythical creatures that guard a dwelling, business, or gravesite. See also *black tortoise, red bird, green dragon,* and *white tiger.*

Landform school: See *Form school.*

lo pan (loh-PAN): The feng shui master's compass, used to determine the directions of auspicious chi in a given location.

lo shu (loh-SHOO): A grid of nine squares, each bearing a number, used in Compass feng shui to divine fortunes. It is also the source for the nine-star ki astrology.

mantra (MAHN-trah): A spiritual chant using sounds and word meaning that is performed to connect the individual's chi to the chi of the universe. See also the *Six True Syllables Mantra* and the *Heart and Mind Calming Mudra.*

meridians: Pathways of chi in the human body. See also *chakras.*

metal: One of the five elements. Metal is precise and conductive. It's associated with autumn, with communication and creativity, and with white and metallic colors.

ming tang: Literally, "bright hall"; an open, inviting space where beneficial chi collects before or upon entering a home, room, or workspace.

monkey: One of the 12 Chinese zodiac animals, associated with the element metal and the hours of 3:00 P.M. to 5:00 P.M. The most recent monkey year was 1992.

nine-star ki: A system of astrology related to feng shui, based on the lo shu square of nine numbers. Each number represents specific attributes, elements, and patterns of luck. Readings of the lo shu square can recommend certain auspicious courses of action or remedies for individuals and households.

ox: One of the 12 Chinese zodiac animals, associated with the element earth and the hours of 1:00 A.M. to 3:00 A.M. The most recent ox year was 1997.

pig: One of the 12 Chinese zodiac animals, associated with the element water and the hours of 9:00 P.M. to 11:00 P.M. The most recent pig year was 1995.

rabbit: One of the 12 Chinese zodiac animals, associated with the element wood and the hours of 5:00 A.M. to 7:00 A.M. The most recent rabbit year was 1999.

rat: One of the 12 Chinese zodiac animals, associated with the element water and the hours of 11:00 P.M. to 1:00 A.M. The most recent rat year was 1996.

red bird: One of the four landform guardians that protect a home or other site. It's also sometimes called the red raven or red phoenix. The red bird is symbolized by a low hill or wall at the front of the site. It is associated with summer.

ren chai: Human luck, or karma—what we do with the luck heaven provides. See also *tien chai* and *ti chai*.

rooster: One of the 12 Chinese zodiac animals, associated with the element metal, and the hours of 5:00 P.M. to 7:00 P.M. The most recent rooster year was 1993.

sha chi: Piercing, harmful chi; also called "killing breath" or "poison arrow."

sheep (also ram or goat): One of the 12 Chinese zodiac animals, associated with the element fire and the hours of 1:00 P.M. to 3:00 P.M. The most recent sheep year was 2003.

ship: A figure or painting of a sailing ship, sometimes laden with gold ingots or other treasure, which is often placed in the home to attract wealth chi.

Six True Syllables Mantra: A sacred chant used to uplift the mind and connect with the spiritual realm. Its syllables, "Om Ma Ni Pad Me Hum," translate loosely as "Hail to the Jewel in the Lotus."

snake: One of the 12 Chinese zodiac animals, associated with the element fire and the hours of 9:00 A.M. to 11:00 A.M. The most recent snake year was 2001.

sying: In Black Hat Sect feng shui, the energy of the mundane, material, logical world (as opposed to yi, the energy of the transcendental and illogical).

tai chi (ty-CHEE): A form of Chinese exercise that conditions the flow of chi in the body. Because it translates literally as "big energy," it is also the term used to refer to the center of the ba-gua, and to the perfect balance of yin and yang forces.

tao (DOW): The patterns of nature; the way of the universe (in contrast to chi, which is the energy of living things).

Ten-Emperors coins: A string of coins bearing the names of ten Chinese emperors, used to protect a home from negative influences and to attract wealth chi.

three-legged toad: A figurine placed in the home to promote luck and wealth.

ti chai (TEE-chy): "Earth luck." The opportunities and patterns of events that find their way to us because of the configuration of our environment. Unlike tien chai, we can influence ti chai directly by the way we arrange our environments. See also *ren chai*.

tien chai (TYEN-chy): "Heaven luck." The luck we were born with. Unlike ren chai and ti chai, we can't change our tien chai, although we can learn to cope with it better and to live according to our destiny.

tiger: One of the 12 Chinese zodiac animals, associated with the element wood and the hours of 3:00 A.M. to 5:00 A.M. The most recent tiger year was 1998.

water: One of the five elements. Water may be deep and still or flowing. It is associated with cleansing, transportation, socializing, and knowledge; also with winter, and with deep blue and black colors.

white tiger: One of the four landform guardians that protect a home or other site. The tiger is located at the right of the site, from the aspect of the front door. It appears as a white outcropping of rock, or other pale landform. It is associated with autumn, and with the protection of wealth.

wood: One of the five elements. Wood is upright and kind. It is associated with springtime, with growth, and with vibrant greens.

Wu Hsing (woo SHING): See *five elements*.

yang: In contrast with yin, the other half of two eternally interactive and opposing energies. Yang energy is male, bright, aggressive, lively, and rising.

yi (YEE): In the Black Hat Sect school of feng shui, the transcendental, illogical aspect of the universe; as opposed to sying, the energy of the mundane, logical world.

yin: In contrast with yang, the other half of two eternally interactive and opposing energies. Yin energy is female, dark, receptive, still, and settling.

Index

Printed in the USA
CPSIA information can be obtained
at www.ICGtesting.com
JSHW012015140824
68134JS00025B/2439